EAT
PLANTS,
B*TCH

GALLERY BOOKS/13A

NEW YORK   LONDON   TORONTO   SYDNEY   NEW DELHI

EAT PLANTS,

**91 VEGAN RECIPES
THAT WILL BLOW YOUR
MEAT-LOVING MIND**

PINKY COLE

13A/Gallery Books
An Imprint of Simon & Schuster, Inc.
1230 Avenue of the Americas
New York, NY 10020

First 13A/Gallery Books hardcover edition November 2022

13A/GALLERY BOOKS and colophon are trademarks of Simon & Schuster, Inc.

For information about special discounts for bulk purchases, please contact Simon & Schuster Special Sales
at 1-866-506-1949 or business@simonandschuster.com.

The Simon & Schuster Speakers Bureau can bring authors to your live event.
For more information or to book an event, contact the Simon & Schuster Speakers Bureau at 1-866-248-3049
or visit our website at www.simonspeakers.com.

Interior design by Ruth Lee-Mui

Photography copyright © 2021 by Madelynne Ross of Bites and Bevs LLC

Food Styling by Madelynne Ross

Manufactured in China

1 3 5 7 9 10 8 6 4 2

Library of Congress Control Number: 2022937815

ISBN 978-1-9821-7831-4
ISBN 978-1-9821-7832-1 (ebook)

This cookbook is dedicated to my children.

*May you always enjoy the art of gathering around food and family
while creating lifelong traditions and memories.*

I hope these recipes continue to keep our family together forever.

viii   Introduction

xii   Black, Vegan, and Cool

xvi   Black Boss Tings

xx   Vegan Pantry Staples

xxiv   Vegan FAQ

188   Acknowledgments

190   Index

CONTENTS

001

ONE

**GOOD MORNING,
GRAND RISING**

025

TWO

**JAMAICAN
SATURDAYS**

069

THREE

**KICK UP
RUMPUS**

111

FOUR

**GOOD OL'
SOUTHERN COMFORT**

155

FIVE

**DA BUTTERS,
DA DIPS,
DA JAMS,
AND DA JELLIES**

175

SIX

**DEM SWEET
THANGS**

INTRODUCTION

*Young Pinky with her mom
and siblings*

I started Slutty Vegan in 2018, and it's interesting because when I look back over my life, I think about all the things that I've done since I was a kid to get to this point. Being vegan was something that was already embedded in me: My mother has been a vegetarian for most of my life. While I've never seen her eat meat, she did have fish occasionally (in the Rastafarian tradition, fish is allowed under a vegetarian diet). My father is a vegetarian as well.

Growing up in a single-parent household, with a woman who was a Jamaican Rastafarian, my siblings and I ate what she ate. We ate a lot of fish, soy products, and vegan Ital food. We were raised with a more conscious way of living and got accustomed to that lifestyle.

As I got older, I realized that I still wanted to live that way. In 2007, I decided to become a full vegetarian. I can remember being in college and everybody looking at me like, "This girl is weird. What's wrong with you? You need some chicken!" But I knew that that wasn't the life that I wanted.

It's funny, in hindsight I see that the universe was guiding me through my vegan journey to set me up for Slutty Vegan. I'm so happy that it happened that way, because what might look like something that happened overnight is actually a success story that has been brewing all of my life. I've always been an entrepreneur. I've always been a hustler. I've always been the person to really take something out of nothing and make it beautiful. I can remember selling chicken sandwiches when I was fourteen. When I was sixteen, I made money by throwing parties. When I was in college, I had a couple side hustles doing hair and being a party promoter. I did everything that you could think of. I would even give people money to flip, whether it was legal or illegal, because I knew that I wanted an opportunity to get my mother out of the situation of being a single parent and having five kids to take care of. When I considered my father, who spent twenty-two years in prison, I just knew that my legacy had to be bigger and better than that.

I had a pop-up restaurant for three years that everybody used to go to, and I sold jerk chicken even though I didn't eat meat. I was telling people it tasted good, but it just wasn't in alignment with who I was. Then I lost that restaurant in 2016 to a grease fire and I thought all was lost. Now I'm glad that it happened because it gave me the knowledge and the education that I needed to be able to open up Slutty Vegan, make some changes, and do things differently.

When I started Slutty Vegan in 2018, I didn't expect it to be anything more than a ghost concept. After I felt good about the concept, I called my best friends, and they said, "Pinky, this is a good idea!" Running with it, I went on the Internet and started looking for recipes and started doing all this crazy stuff—and it worked.

Pretty soon, Snoop Dogg ate my first vegan burger, then Jermaine Dupri and Lil Duval, and then everything literally went up from there. I'm so grateful for how things happen in life. I truly believe that everything happens for a reason. That belief is really what allowed me to be able to create opportunities for myself and for other people.

Since 2018, I've been able to open up three brick-and-mortar locations and two food trucks. I've been on tour in over twenty states with our food truck to test the market and get people excited about the brand. I've done partnerships with Shake Shack, Incogmeato, Rap Snacks, and Impossible

Pinky cutting the ribbon at the grand opening of her restaurant in Jonesboro, Georgia

Foods. I've been able to leverage other people's platforms to take my brand to the next level. What makes Slutty Vegan beautiful is that we make good food. Vegan or not, we make good food, and people can appreciate it. When people, especially our people, eat good food, it's enjoyable.

I'm happy that people who were never interested in veganism are willing to try it because of Slutty Vegan. When you come to Slutty Vegan, you come for the experience and you leave with the food, and we make that necessary. We make a point of that because everyone wants a place to go to that offers not only a good experience but also great customer service and great food. We tied all those things together and are now bringing some of the great recipes from Slutty Vegan to you in this book.

When I started writing and compiling the recipes for *Eat Plants, B*tch,* I wanted to create something that would meet people where they are. These recipes are for flexitarians. I'm not pushing my agenda on you. I'm simply telling you that you have some options. You can throw some vegan items on your typical menu. This book is dedicated to all of the people who might not want to be vegan but who want choices that actually taste good.

Doing this book is important to me because seeing how unhealthy we are as a people, I know the power of food. Food brings people together. Food connects people on a greater level than you could ever imagine. I am doing what Martin Luther King, Jr. was able to do with Black people and white people: bring them together. But in this case, I'm bringing people together in the name of food. I'm happy that I'm able to do that.

BLACK, VEGAN, AND COOL

Pinky during a MorningStar Farms Incogmeato Chik'n Tenders launch event in Atlanta

What does veganism mean to me? Veganism means being able to find self-love within, being mindful of what you consume and having love for the earth and for the animals. To emotionally, spiritually, mentally live better. If you can live better, then you think better, you communicate better, you love better, and you have better relationships.

What makes me happiest is to see so many Black people adopting this lifestyle, whether they believe it's trendy or not. Because for so long, statistically, studies have shown that Black people die from high cholesterol and diabetes at a higher rate than other nationalities. Obviously, I'm no nutritionist, but what I do know is this: Vegan cheeseburgers are way better for us than animal flesh.

In addition to my insights, I thought it would be great for you to hear what it means to be Black, Vegan, and Cool from some of my favorite fellow vegan chefs. Check out what they have to say about what it means to transition to and adopt a vegan lifestyle and some of the benefits to their bodies and their lives.

TIPS FROM BLACK VEGAN CHEFS

I think that veganism is easy. It's not hard at all. It requires you to use your imagination, but veganism is something that can be easily achieved if you really put your mind to it, whether you do it for your health or you do it for the animals. Whatever you do it for, I believe that living a plant-based/vegan lifestyle will offer you many benefits. Some people lose weight from going vegan. Some people just feel smarter, feel lighter, live longer. But for me, I just wanted to be more conscious. I'm always trying to find new ways to be better than the last version of myself.

My advice for anyone going vegan is to start simple: Veganize your staples first, such as pasta, sandwiches, soups, and burgers. Never compromise flavor. After all, you don't eat unseasoned meat, so don't eat unseasoned veggies! **—ERIN WELLS, AKA THAT CHOCOLATE VEGAN**

For those considering transitioning to veganism, it's important to understand that being a vegan is not a diet, it's a lifestyle choice. I suggest taking the transition slowly and really take the time to educate yourself on what you're putting into your body. Your body is your temple! I also encourage you to enjoy the process. Try new things and really get in touch with yourself. Yes, there are going to be days when you have setbacks and indulge in that chocolate cake—but then get back to it. I promise the way you will feel both mentally and spiritually is much more rewarding! **—CHEF QUAN**

Research is KEY! There are unlimited plant-based options that you must learn. Educate yourself about universal seasonings, spices, and herbs.

— CHEF EL-AMIN

Try new fruits and veggies. A great place to start is the Asian market. Asian grocery stores have a global assortment of goodies. There are eighty thousand edible plants on the planet. Most people will only experience 5 percent or less just based on geographical location and proximity to fresh produce. The more veggies you like, the fewer animals you eat. Eat cultural foods. American food is very meat centered. However, this is not the case for many exotic cultures. My top picks are Ethiopian, Thai, Mediterranean, and Indian restaurants. They are also super clutch because they exist in every city. With this perspective a delicious WELL-SEASONED vegan meal is always around the corner. **— SUNNI SPEAKS**

BLACK
BOSS
TINGS

When I asked some of my favorite fellow vegan chefs to share some of their favorite recipes for this book, I wasn't expecting them to also come back to me with amazing advice about what it means to be an entrepreneur. In addition to packing this book with my favorite recipes of theirs, I thought it would be a beautiful thing to share with you some of their wisdom about what it has meant for them to create their own businesses, particularly in the food and service industry. So many people in our industry have been severely impacted by the COVID-19 crisis and struggled to keep their restaurants, food trucks, and catering services going. Even if you aren't in the food industry, as a self-made woman entrepreneur, I thought that this would be the perfect way to show you what it means to be a Black boss and give you some good insight from people who have been there, done that, and can inspire you to go after your biggest dreams.

For any entrepreneur entering the culinary space, I encourage you to push yourself to have a fearless mindset. Working as an independent chef, I've learned that the fear of failure does more damage to your brand than not accepting a challenging opportunity that could potentially take you to the next level. All you need is that one look! Whenever you face adversity, I challenge you to dig deep and believe in yourself; find your way through any obstacles you may face. The road less traveled will not be smooth, however, as long as you stay true to your purpose and remain diligent, the reward will be worth every second of the work you put in. —**CHEF QUAN**

I think that one of our biggest accomplishments was being able to bounce back after our falls. We've had two big falls where we lost our credibility: We grew so fast that we weren't able to meet the needs, so no one wanted to do service or business with us. It was pretty bad . . . but because we knew our purpose, we got back up and rebuilt trust and credibility, and the trust of the people.

We gained better customer service and now the business is flourishing. We see our business going to a place where we are able to reach people and make them feel good about making better choices. We're not religious food bullies but more or less your Cleansing Saints.

We will have a warehouse where we will test and produce our own supplements, our own protein, our own detox teas. We will sell these in stores across America so people can start to understand the benefit and the beauty of a cleanse, and we are going to be your one-stop shop for being able to do that. We want to be able to appeal to the vegan, to the nonvegan, to the health-conscious, and to those who are clueless. We understand the beauty of moderation over deprivation and want all to have as healthy a lifestyle as possible.

My tidbit for success as an entrepreneur would be to never give up. Consistency is key and no matter what, know your purpose. When you go in knowing the why, the what and the how will always catch up with you.

—**CRYSTAL SHAE BARNWELL**

Leap and the net will appear. Many of us feel that so many things have to be right or perfect in order to "jump off the porch" with our endeavors. But faith without works is dead. So we must have faith, but also move, because whatever entity we believe in will only meet us halfway in movement as well as effort. You are never broke until you run out of network. Keeping good people around your business is key. Managing our business relationships is absolutely critical to success. Without favors being done or owed, many businesses would fail almost immediately. People don't buy your product from you; they buy how you make them feel about your product. Everything a person buys, whether product or service, is based on their experience. It's absolutely essential to make sure that every person who comes in contact with your product, service, or brand has a stellar experience. **—SUNNI SPEAKS**

For any upcoming entrepreneurs I would say try to be consistent in delivering quality and creative content. Also never measure your success by anyone else's. Everyone has their own path to success. **—CULINARY GROOVE**

To be successful as an entrepreneur is to never give up. There will be doors slammed again and again, but keep going until you can kick one down!
—ERIN WELLS, AKA THAT CHOCOLATE VEGAN

It's okay to reroute—just make sure you STAY on track! **—CIERRA BROOKS**

Destiny is not a place; destiny is a PURPOSE to be reached. The two most important days of your life are the day you were born and the day you find out WHY you were born. **—CHEF EL-AMIN**

VEGAN PANTRY STAPLES

How do you get started with making sure that you can cook the amazing recipes that you're about to discover in this book? No worries, I got you covered. In this chapter, I am breaking down my favorite vegan staples that'll help you get some basic oils in your pantry; put in some good nut butters, nondairy milks, and cheeses; and learn how to use some great substitutes for your favorite baking and everyday recipes.

OILS

HIGH OLEIC SAFFLOWER OIL. Perfect for higher-temperature cooking, since the oil is resistant to scorching.

OLIVE OIL. Good for general low-temperature cooking. Always buy "extra-virgin," and try to get it unfiltered if possible. Unrefined olive oil offers a strong, peppery flavor that, together with balsamic vinegar, is a wonderful dip for freshly baked breads.

SESAME OIL. An inexpensive way to jazz up any dish, especially stir-fried vegetables and Asian-style noodles. Sesame oil has a very low scorching point, so it's best to add it to your food right before serving. The flavors are strong, so just a squirt of oil goes a long way.

UNREFINED COCONUT OIL. Perfect for dishes with delicate flavors. Coconut oil also perfectly complements the flavor of most vegetables.

NUT BUTTERS, MILKS, AND CHEESES

NUTS AND NUT BUTTERS. Keep a variety of roasted whole nuts on hand; they make a great vegan snack. And check the recipes for specific nuts, like almonds and cashews, which can be purchased raw or roasted and sliced, chopped, or whole.

There are also a number of ways to add nuts to your diet besides eating them whole. One obvious way is to purchase nut butters. While peanut butter is by far the most popular such product, any nut can be ground into butter. Almond, cashew, and hazelnut butters are widely available. Many natural foods stores also stock macadamia nut butter and pistachio butter.

Nut butters are good for far more than just sandwich spreads—they're also an incredibly versatile cooking ingredient.

NONDAIRY MILKS. Nondairy milks come in a variety of options. You'll see coconut, almond, and oat in my recipes but there are plenty more, from pea milk to rice milk. Take your time and see which milk works best for you and your family.

VEGAN CHEESES. Like nondairy milks, the world of vegan cheeses is massive. Whatever you're looking for, you can find it. Need shredded mozzarella, sharp cheddar, American? There is a nondairy option; check your local supermarket or health food store.

EGG REPLACEMENTS

APPLESAUCE. Using applesauce is a fat-free way to replace eggs in baked goods. Use ¼ cup of unsweetened applesauce to replace each egg in a recipe. In addition to reducing calories, this vegan egg replacer adds moisture and flavor to cookies, cakes, muffins, and breads.

FLAXSEED. For each egg in a recipe, combine 1 tablespoon of ground flaxseed with 3 tablespoons of water, stir to combine, and let stand for

5 minutes to thicken. Ground flaxseed emulates eggs' binding qualities in breads, cakes, muffins, cookies, burgers, and vegan meatballs.

RIPE BANANAS. Ripe bananas work as a vegan egg substitute by adding moisture to plant-based recipes, while also imparting sweetness. However, be sure to add more of the leavening agent (such as baking powder) to avoid dense baked goods. Ripe bananas are best suited for cakes, pancakes, and brownies. Use 1 ripe medium banana, mashed up, to replace each egg in a recipe.

TOFU, SILKEN AND FIRM. Tofu is a protein-packed vegan egg substitute. Soft silken tofu adds a creamy texture when used as an egg substitute in cheesecakes, ice cream, sour cream, or puddings. Firm tofu is a great option for egg-free cooking, and works best in savory dishes such as eggless quiches, lasagna, vegan egg salad, or a breakfast scramble. A quarter cup of pureed silken tofu can be used to replace each egg in a recipe.

TAPIOCA STARCH. Tapioca starch is used as a binding or thickening agent for sauces, puddings, and condiments. Use 1 tablespoon of tapioca starch, blended with 3 teaspoons of water, to replace each egg in a recipe.

CHICKPEA FLOUR. High in protein, chickpea flour works as both a binding and raising agent and is one of the best natural egg replacements in baked goods, such as scones, cookies, and biscotti. With a surprisingly similar texture and flavor to eggs, chickpea flour has also become a common egg substitute in omelets and quiches. For each egg in a recipe, mix 3 tablespoons of chickpea flour with 3 tablespoons of water until it combines to a thick and creamy paste.

VEGAN
FAQ

WHAT DOES IT MEAN TO BE VEGAN?

To me, being vegan means being compassionate to all forms of life. I have made the choice to eliminate all animal products from my life and diet. A Slutty Vegan, in my mind, is someone who eats vegan but enjoys junk food—as long as it's not dead. I chose that name for my business because I knew it would be a great hook and help people to reimagine food. What I didn't know was how much of an impact it would make in the long run.

WHAT IS THE DIFFERENCE BETWEEN BEING A VEGAN AND A VEGETARIAN?

Vegetarians do not eat meat but still consume animal by-products like milk, cheese, eggs, etc. Vegans make the choice to forego any meat or animal products.

WHY DID YOU DECIDE TO BECOME VEGAN?

I was one of those people who would always try to raise awareness about the impact diet has on health, and how and why heart disease and type 2 diabetes are so prevalent in the Black community. People of color suffer and die from chronic diseases and lifestyle diseases at a disproportionately higher rate than any other race or community. I think that really inspired me to cut out animal products. My mother was also a big inspiration to me when it comes to maintaining a healthy, plant-based diet.

WHAT WERE SOME OF THE GREATEST BENEFITS YOU'VE GAINED FROM A PLANT-BASED DIET?

I think that my diet played a large part in setting me up for success. There was a point in my life, when I'd moved back to Atlanta for good, when I was really focused on myself. I was running, getting my mind together, eating a vegan diet, and mentally preparing for something big that I knew was coming, and it just so happened that Slutty Vegan was right around the corner.

WHAT IS THE BEST WAY TO START EXPERIMENTING WITH A PLANT-BASED DIET?

I think healthy eating means eating what makes you feel good! We know that things like vegetables and quinoa are a big part of most vegans' diets, but who says you can't enjoy a great burger every now and again, too? There are lots of great plant-based burgers (and pizza and "chicken" nuggets and . . .) out there, so I suggest starting with vegan versions of the foods you know and love. Food isn't just about feeding your body, it's also about nourishing your soul. Being healthy means being able to take time away from your busy life to indulge in the little pleasures, and there's no greater pleasure than eating good food with good people.

HOW DO I FIND VEGAN ITEMS IN A SUPERMARKET?

The best way to find vegan options in a supermarket is to read signs and labels. Many markets have aisles dedicated to plant-based or vegan foods, or group those items together. If your local market doesn't have a dedicated aisle, check for food packaging with labels that say "plant-based" or "vegan." You can also read ingredient lists to ensure items do not contain dairy or meat products.

HOW CAN I FIND VEGAN RESTAURANTS?

The internet is your friend! Search "vegan food" and the name of the city you are in or traveling to, and some options should pop up. You can also check websites like Happycow.Net and even Yelp. Sometimes you may find it hard to find a 100 percent vegan restaurant. If that's the case, you can check with your server or ask to speak to the chef. The chef can usually whip up something tasty without using dairy or meat products. You will find some great vegan options while dining out this way.

WILL A PLANT-BASED DIET HELP ME MANAGE CHRONIC ILLNESSES, SUCH AS DIABETES OR HIGH BLOOD PRESSURE?

Veganism has several health benefits and can contribute to an overall quality of life, including helping to manage illnesses, etc.

HOW CAN I GET MY KIDS OR MY SIGNIFICANT OTHER TO TRY NEW VEGAN DISHES?

Make the things they like, and make them delicious! I believe I can make anything taste good. To do that, I use fresh herbs to spice up all of my meals, as well as pimentos, coconut milk, Jamaican peppers, fresh garlic, vegetable bouillon, exotic mushrooms, and more. Most of our consumers at Slutty Vegan are meat eaters. My core audience is meat eaters. I'm intentional about that. Vegans have already made the conscious decision not to eat meat, but the meat eaters are the people I really want to speak to. They are the ones you need to persuade to want healthier options, even if it starts at vegan versions of comfort foods and being more conscious about animals.

ONE

GOOD MORNING, GRAND RISING

Like most '80s babies, I grew up looking forward to Saturday mornings, when I could watch my favorite cartoon shows such as *The Smurfs*, *Alvin and the Chipmunks*, and *Jem and the Holograms*. Nothing went better with Saturday morning cartoons than a big old bowl of cereal, and whole milk dribbling down my chin.

While I have definitely traded in the dairy milk for my favorite nut milks and other plant-based goodies, I've discovered that breakfast can be just as fun and exciting as a grown-up vegan as it was for me in my childhood days. As my empire continues to grow and I've got a new baby girl in my life, I now realize just how important it is to start out my day with power fuel that'll keep me going for hours on end.

I love the recipes in this chapter because they are very easy, can be prepared in advance, and will definitely give you good energy throughout your morning without that midmorning slump of weaning off your caffeine or experiencing a rough carbohydrate crash. Some of my favorite recipes in this chapter, and ones that I recommend for those of you who are just starting out on your vegan journey, are the Berry Smoothie (page 5), the Avocado "Bacon" Pastry Bites (page 2)—which I love making in bulk and warming up throughout the week—the Fresh Fig Toasts (page 3), and if you've got some time on a Saturday and a Sunday morning, I highly recommend the Spicy Sausage Gravy and Biscuits (page 20). This is a good old Southern breakfast classic that'll keep you full and your mouth watering for more.

AVOCADO "BACON" PASTRY BITES

Serves 4

These pastry bites combine the best of avocado toast and vegan bacon into a quick breakfast treat that will be satisfying for you and your whole household.

2 teaspoons Slut Dust or your favorite all-purpose seasoning blend
1 teaspoon smoked paprika
¼ teaspoon ground cumin
¼ teaspoon coarsely ground black pepper
¼ teaspoon salt
4 strips vegan bacon, such as Slutty Strips

2 tablespoons extra-virgin olive oil
1 firm, ripe avocado
1½ tablespoons fresh lime juice
4 slices multigrain bread, lightly toasted
4 romaine lettuce leaves, washed and thoroughly dried
2 Roma (plum) tomatoes, sliced

IN a small bowl, combine the Slut Dust, smoked paprika, cumin, pepper, and ⅛ teaspoon of the salt. Using half the mixture, sprinkle one side of the bacon slices.

LINE a plate with paper towels. In a large nonstick skillet, heat the olive oil over medium heat. Arrange the bacon in a single layer, spice-side down. Sprinkle the strips with the remaining spice mixture. Cook until golden brown, about 4 minutes. Flip the strips over and continue cooking for another minute. Remove from the heat and transfer the bacon strips to the paper towels to absorb any excess oil. Set aside to cool slightly.

MEANWHILE, halve and pit the avocado. Scoop the flesh into a bowl and mash it with a fork until creamy. Add the lime juice and remaining ⅛ teaspoon salt and mix well

TO assemble the toasts, spread some mashed avocado on each slice of bread and top with the lettuce, tomatoes, and bacon.

FRESH FIG TOASTS

Makes 24 toasts

You might only associate figs with your favorite Fig Newtons from back in the day, but this classy upgrade, a perfect addition to your small-plate platter, a Sunday brunch, or a weekday morning with the fam, will elevate your palate and impress your crew.

1 loaf vegan baguette
¼ cup extra-virgin olive oil
¼ teaspoon freshly ground black pepper
6 ounces vegan cream cheese
1 teaspoon fresh lime juice
½ teaspoon fresh lemon juice

4 ounces sliced roasted almonds
½ cup roasted cashews, crushed
12 fresh figs, rinsed and patted dry
6 tablespoons agave syrup
6 tablespoons golden raisins
½ cup chopped chives

PREHEAT the oven to 375°F.

SLICE the baguette crosswise on an angle to form 24 crostini and toss with the olive oil to coat. Arrange on a baking sheet and bake until golden brown, 7 to 10 minutes.

SPRINKLE the pepper on top of the crostini and set aside.

IN a medium bowl, mix together the cream cheese, lime juice, and lemon juice until well incorporated.

SPREAD the cream cheese mixture over the crostini and top with the sliced almonds and crushed cashews.

SLICE the figs in half through the stem and place cut side up on the crostini. Drizzle with the agave syrup, top with the raisins and chives, and serve.

BERRY SMOOTHIE

Serves 2 or 3

This satisfying smoothie is filled with seasonal berries and supercharged seeds and minerals. A glass of this is a great way to jump-start your morning and keep you full for hours to come.

1 cup organic blueberries or mixed berries, fresh or frozen, plus more for garnish
1 small ripe banana, sliced and frozen
3 tablespoons coconut or almond milk
1 tablespoon unsweetened shredded coconut
1 tablespoon chia seeds
1 tablespoon flaxseed
1 teaspoon agave syrup
1 scoop plain or vanilla protein powder (optional)

IN a blender combine the berries and frozen banana and pulse on low for 45 to 60 seconds.

ADD the milk, shredded coconut, chia seeds, flaxseed, agave syrup, and protein powder, if desired, and pulse on low until it is smooth and creamy.

POUR into glasses and top with more berries, if desired, and serve.

BLACKER BERRY, SWEETER JUICE

Serves 1 or 2

There's no better way to get your morning started than to supercharge your day with the anti-oxidant fighting power of blueberries and blackberries, a potassium blast from a ripe banana, and a handful of fresh mint leaves to wake up your palate. And if you're not familiar with alkaline water, it has added electrolytes and minerals and more good stuff—and it's often carbon neutral! It's the only water I drink, and I serve it in my restaurants. This is an easy, on-the-go juice that will keep you cranking throughout your morning.

1 ripe banana, cut into ¼-inch-thick rounds
½ cup blueberries
½ cup blackberries
½ cup fresh mint leaves
1 cup alkaline water

IN a blender, combine the banana, blueberries, blackberries, mint leaves, and alkaline water, and blend.

POUR into a glass and serve.

ENJOY!

BLUEBERRY SUNSHINE SMOOTHIE

Serves 1 or 2

Beat the morning blues with a kick of citrus in this refreshing smoothie that will fuel, revive, and energize you for the day ahead.

1 ripe banana, fresh or frozen
1 cup organic mixed berries, fresh or frozen
1 cup wild blueberries, fresh or frozen
½ cup diced green apple, fresh or frozen
½ cup almond milk yogurt
¼ cup freshly squeezed orange juice, plus more if needed
¼ cup agave syrup
Granola and sliced fruit of your choice (optional)

IN a blender, combine the banana, mixed berries, blueberries, apple, yogurt, and orange juice. Blend slowly. Add a small splash of orange juice if needed.

TRANSFER the mixture to a bowl or glass. If desired, top with granola and sliced fruit.

CARAMEL MOCHA ICED "COFFEE"

Serves 2 or 3

You don't have to depend on Starbucks for your early-morning jolt. My iced "coffee" contains the energy boost you need without the caffeine jitters. This unique blend of cashews, carob powder, dates, and flaxseed will have you ditching your morning coffee for this delightful drink in no time. You can make your "coffee" thicker by using less water and/or ice, or thinner by using more.

½ cup vegan caramel, plus more for garnish
2 cups water
¾ cup chopped dates
⅔ cup raw or roasted cashews

¼ cup Cafix (caffeine-free grain beverage)
2 tablespoons carob powder
2 tablespoons ground flaxseed
1½ cups ice

IN a blender, combine the caramel, water, dates, cashews, Cafix, carob powder, and flaxseed and blend thoroughly, 45 to 60 seconds.

ADD the ice and blend for 10 to 15 seconds more.

DRIZZLE caramel on the inside of a glass for garnish and let it run down the sides before adding the "iced" coffee.

ENJOY!

CHI CHI'S VEGAN CHURRO WAFFLES

Serves 4 to 6

The deets from the chef: Inspired by the popular Mexican street snack churros and my love for waffles, this breakfast pays homage to Mexican culture as well as my Southern American roots. Serve these warm with your favorite toppings. My favorites are maple syrup, fruit, and vegan whipped cream.

CHURRO COATING:
1 cup sugar
2 tablespoons ground cinnamon
½ cup vegan butter, melted

WAFFLE BATTER:
2 cups unsweetened nondairy milk
¼ cup coconut oil
1 tablespoon pure vanilla extract
2 teaspoons fresh lemon juice
2 cups all-purpose flour
2 tablespoons baking powder
1 tablespoon sugar
½ tablespoon ground cinnamon
½ tablespoon ground nutmeg
½ teaspoon salt
Cooking spray

MAKE THE CHURRO COATING: In a small bowl, mix the sugar and cinnamon together. Spread onto a large plate. Set aside. Set the melted butter aside.

MAKE THE WAFFLE BATTER: In a medium bowl, stir together the milk, oil, vanilla, and lemon juice. Set aside for 5 minutes to create vegan buttermilk.

MEANWHILE, into a large bowl, sift together the flour, baking powder, sugar, cinnamon, nutmeg, and salt.

POUR the liquid mixture into the dry ingredients and gently mix. Small lumps are okay. Don't overmix.

PREHEAT a waffle maker and mist with cooking spray. Add batter and follow the manufacturer's instructions for a crispy waffle.

REMOVE the waffle and brush with the melted butter on both sides. Dip both sides of the waffle in the churro coating.

REPEAT until all the batter and churro coating are used. Serve immediately.

ENJOY!

GARDEN SCRAMBLE

Serves 2 or 3

You don't have to settle for boring egg whites with this recipe. This completely vegan scramble will wake up your morning with fresh onions, celery, Roma tomatoes, and mushrooms.

2 tablespoons safflower oil
½ cup diced onion
⅓ cup diced celery
½ cup diced mushrooms
½ pound firm tofu
⅓ cup diced Roma (plum) tomatoes

½ cup shredded vegan cheese
½ teaspoon Himalayan pink salt
½ teaspoon freshly cracked black pepper
Green onions, chopped, for garnish

IN a large skillet, heat the oil over medium heat. Add the onion and celery and cook, stirring occasionally, until translucent, about 10 minutes. Add the mushrooms and cook until tender, about 10 minutes.

ADD the tofu, breaking it up into small pieces, and cook for 3 minutes. Add the tomatoes and cook for 6 minutes more. Stir in the cheese, and season with the salt and pepper. Serve garnished with the green onions.

ENJOY!

MORNING RELEASE

Serves 2

The perfect way to take your body from sluggish to energized, the Morning Release has healthy chunks of mango, spinach, banana, hemp hearts, flaxseed, and oats. This recipe is going to deliver on its promise, so just make sure you're not too far from home when its power starts to kick in. If you'd like, make your Morning Release ahead of time; it can be stored, covered, in the fridge for up to a day.

1½ cups unsweetened almond milk
1 cup mango chunks, plus more for garnish
1 cup fresh spinach leaves, plus more for garnish
1 ripe banana

1 ounce hemp hearts
1 teaspoon flaxseed, plus more for garnish
1 cup rolled oats
Ice (optional)

IN a blender, combine the almond milk, mango chunks, spinach, banana, hemp hearts, flaxseed, and oats and . . . well . . . BLEND!

DON'T even waste time on a cup. Just drink it straight from the blender! But if you do want to keep it classy, serve this smoothie over ice, if desired, in an 8- to 10-ounce glass. Garnish with a few mango chunks sprinkled with flaxseed and a spinach leaf.

PARSLEY MOSS SMOOTHIE

Serves 1 or 2

The secret ingredient here is sea moss, which you've likely had even if you didn't know it at the time. It's used in many foods as a binding agent. So, sea moss with banana and avocado here—let's get our gut together!

¾ cup plus 2 tablespoons coconut water

Handful of parsley, plus a couple of sprigs for garnish

¾ cup ice

1 ripe banana, sliced

½ avocado, pitted

1 jumbo Medjool date, pitted

2 tablespoons sea moss gel

1 tablespoon agave syrup

1 tablespoon hemp hearts

1 tablespoon lucuma powder

½ teaspoon moringa powder

IN a blender, combine the coconut water, parsley, and ice and blend. Add the banana, avocado, date, sea moss gel, agave syrup, hemp hearts, lucuma powder, and moringa powder and blend until smooth. Pour into a glass and garnish with a sprig of parsley. Serve immediately.

PAN-ROASTED PB&J

Serves 2

Ain't nothing like reliving your childhood favorites, especially when it comes to a good peanut butter and jelly sandwich. This PB&J gets grown and sexy with a little time in a hot skillet to warm the peanut butter and add a crunchier crust to your favorite bread.

¼ cup vegan mayonnaise
⅔ cup crunchy peanut butter

⅓ cup roasted red pepper jam
4 slices vegan sourdough bread

SPREAD the mayonnaise on one side of the bread slices. Spread the peanut butter and jam on the other side of the bread slices. Close up the sandwiches.

HEAT a large skillet over medium heat. Add the sandwiches and cook until golden brown, about 1 minute. Flip the sandwiches and cook until golden brown on the second side and the peanut butter is nice and gooey, about 1 minute.

SERVE immediately and enjoy.

SPICY SAUSAGE GRAVY AND BISCUITS

Serves 10

My name is Chef Nikki In The Mix and I'm an Atlanta-based vegan chef. I went vegan in 2016 after I saw footage of what happens inside a slaughterhouse. It was heartbreaking to see the animals being slaughtered and I was disgusted. At that moment, I made the decision to stop eating meat. It challenged me to re-create some of my favorite dishes I grew up enjoying, but without the meat and dairy. This eventually led me to vegan cooking and one of my biggest accomplishments to date, creating my own vegan pancake mix: Nikki's Fat Ass Cakes!

As an entrepreneur, I have grown to trust and learn from "the process." Same with veganism. If you are starting out, go at your own pace. This is your journey and no one else's. Veganism is about making better decisions, not perfection.

1 (8.3-ounce) package vegan spicy breakfast sausage patties
2 tablespoons grapeseed oil
¼ cup all-purpose flour
2½ cups unsweetened almond milk
½ teaspoon Louisiana hot sauce
½ teaspoon vegan Worcestershire sauce
½ teaspoon freshly ground black pepper, plus more for garnish
½ teaspoon salt
⅛ teaspoon cayenne pepper
10 Biscuits (page 22), freshly made
Parsley, chopped, for garnish

IN a large skillet, cook the sausage over medium-high heat according to the package directions.

TRANSFER the cooked sausage to a bowl and, when it's cool enough to handle, crumble into pieces by hand.

ADD the oil to the pan. Sprinkle in the flour and whisk for 2 minutes.

POUR in the milk and whisk to combine. Add the hot sauce, Worcestershire sauce, black pepper, salt, and cayenne pepper and simmer, whisking constantly, until thickened and smooth, 8 to 10 minutes.

SERVE immediately over the warm split biscuits, garnished with black pepper and chopped parsley.

Continued on next page

BISCUITS

Makes 10 biscuits

¾ cup unsweetened almond milk
½ teaspoon apple cider vinegar
2 cups all-purpose flour, plus more for
  dusting
1½ tablespoons sugar

1 tablespoon baking powder
½ teaspoon baking soda
1 teaspoon salt
⅓ cup grapeseed oil
Vegan butter, for serving

PREHEAT the oven to 450°F. Line a large baking sheet with parchment paper or a silicone baking mat.

IN a measuring cup, combine the almond milk and vinegar and set aside.

IN a large bowl, whisk together the flour, sugar, baking powder, baking soda, and salt. Add the grapeseed oil and almond milk/vinegar mixture and stir by hand. Gently work it until the dough starts to come together.

TRANSFER the dough to a lightly floured surface. Pat the dough gently to flatten into a square and fold it in thirds. Repeat this process two more times.

PRESS the dough out into a square. Use a 2.5-inch biscuit cutter or drinking glass to cut out the biscuits. Gather any scrap pieces of dough, patting it back down to form a square, and cut out biscuits until you have 10.

ARRANGE the biscuits on the prepared baking sheet touching each other.

BAKE at 450°F until lightly golden brown, 12 to 14 minutes.

BRUSH the tops with butter and serve.

TWO
JAMAICAN
SATURDAYS

In my personal life, I make sure to routinely pause and gather with my village—my family, my closest friends, and the Slutty Vegan leadership team. To do that, we established weekly celebrations known as "Jamaican Saturdays." On these occasions, we potluck—sharing our favorite foods, cleaning the house, and winding down from weekly stressors. There's always plenty of food and drinks. This has helped me to remain connected to my cultural roots and to not stay in work mode. Most important, I believe that gathering keeps us connected and feeling supported. This is especially crucial in our industry, where there are high levels of burnout and fatigue among restaurateurs.

In this chapter, I offer my favorite foods for Jamaican cultural gatherings, and I hope that you will enjoy sharing them with your loved ones. First up is the Beet-tini (page 29). I am a lover of beets in any form really, and I drink beets all the time for their energy and nutrients. I like beets in my morning shakes, and in my cocktails (or mocktails) at night. The Beet-tini is my version of the martini. It is vibrant and can be enjoyed with or without alcohol. Its rich color is sure to be a conversation starter among guests. My only caution is to be aware that beets may stain your teeth initially, so please keep a glass of water nearby. Of course, no gathering is complete without Rum Punch (page 45). This drink reminds me of being home in Jamaica, relaxing on the beach and enjoying the peaceful island vibes. It is a traditional fruit cocktail that tastes best with fresh orange, lime, and pineapple juices.

I also share my favorite savory dishes here, including my Jamaican-style Pineapple Rice Bowl (page 55). I enjoy fresh pineapple, so this infused starch is always satisfying. If you are shopping at a Caribbean or organic grocer, I encourage you to also experiment with different varieties of pineapple for this dish. In Jamaica, the varieties of Sugar Loaf, Cowboy, Ripley, and Smooth Cayenne are grown, and they range from very sweet to tart. In addition, pineapple flesh is not very fibrous, so its juices can serve as a marinade when added to the other ingredients. If you are looking to add even more texture, this dish works well with added vegan shrimp marinated in jerk sauce.

For those who aren't vegan, I included some meals that won't make guests miss meat during a gathering. First up is Paella with Vegan Shrimp (page 52) made with Spanish paella rice. Although this recipe is primarily a seafood dish, my version incorporates vegan bacon and vegan chorizo for texture. In this case, the paella can be made in so many variations, including with vegetables, beans, different rices (like black rice), and other seasonings.

No gathering is complete without foods that honor the land. For example, you can't go wrong with a veggie kebab. Feel free to explore your local farmers' market and modify the dish to your preference. This dish is especially good for anyone you know who may be practicing a raw diet. I go on a raw diet at the start of every year to cleanse my energy and my body. In this instance, I simply add the raw chopped veggies to my salad while guests enjoyed the char-grilled veggies. It's a dish you can't go wrong with.

BEET-TINI

Makes 2 cocktails

A party ain't a party without my legendary Beet-tinis! I know some of you might be wrinkling up your nose at the thought of a cocktail infused with such a strong, earthy vegetable like a beet. But I promise you that after one taste of this cocktail, it will become a staple for all your summer hangouts.

4 ounces triple-distilled vegan vodka
½ small beet, peeled and diced
2 ounces fresh pineapple juice
Ice

OPTIONAL GARNISHES:
2 raw beet slices
4 small pineapple spears
2 beet leaves

IN a glass or bowl, combine the vodka and diced beet. Refrigerate for at least 4 hours and up to overnight to allow the beet juice to bleed into the vodka.

STRAIN the vodka into a bowl (discard the beet).

IN a cocktail shaker, combine the beet vodka, pineapple juice, and ice and shake vigorously for about 30 seconds or until the shaker is cold to the touch.

POUR the mixture into cold martini glasses and add any desired garnishes.

SIP SLOW and enjoy!

CHICKPEA SUNRISE

Serves 4 to 6

Growing up in a household where my grandfather and mother were the chefs of the family, I always wanted to follow their lead and help out in the kitchen wherever I could. As I grew older and lived on my own, I took on a deeper interest in cooking for myself and friends, as good food is always a recipe for bringing people together. I have never actually worked in a restaurant, but I have always tried to bring restaurant quality to the meals I make, so I began posting pictures of my dishes on social media. Then I was encouraged by a handful of friends to create a page solely for showcasing my creations, and from there I took the leap hosting my own events to deliver luxury private-dining experiences.

As I continued to cook and post my meals, I received multiple inquiries about creating dishes to cater to the vegan community. I took on this challenge, as cooking vegan meals was something I had never considered. Recognizing the need to live a cleaner and healthier lifestyle and with the help of a close friend, I made the decision to include a variety of plant-based options in my diet, which has proven to be rewarding for both my health and personal development.

CHICKPEAS:
2 tablespoons extra-virgin olive oil
1 medium onion, chopped
5 garlic cloves, minced
1 large red bell pepper, chopped
1 Scotch bonnet pepper, chopped
2 tablespoons curry powder
1 tablespoon ground turmeric
1 teaspoon grated fresh ginger
1 teaspoon ground allspice
1 teaspoon sweet paprika
3 sprigs fresh thyme
Salt and freshly ground black pepper
3 cups vegetable broth
1 (15-ounce) can coconut milk
2 (16-ounce) cans chickpeas, drained and rinsed
3 tablespoons cornstarch (optional)

COCONUT RICE:
2 cups vegetable broth
1 (15-ounce) can coconut milk
2 cups long-grain white rice

MANGO SALSA:
2 firm, ripe mangoes, diced
1 avocado, pitted and diced
1 red bell pepper, chopped
½ red onion, diced
3 tablespoons finely chopped fresh cilantro
Salt and freshly ground black pepper

PLANTAINS:
Canola oil
2 ripe plantains, peeled and sliced into 1-inch rounds
Cilantro, chopped, for garnish

MAKE THE CHICKPEAS: In a large heavy-bottomed saucepan or Dutch oven, heat the olive oil over medium heat. Add the onion and cook, stirring, until translucent, about 5 minutes.

Continued on next page

ADD the garlic, bell pepper, and Scotch bonnet pepper and cook until aromatic.

STIR in the curry powder, turmeric, ginger, allspice, paprika, thyme, and salt and black pepper to taste and cook for a few minutes.

ADD the broth and coconut milk and bring to a boil. Stir in the chickpeas and cook over medium-low heat, stirring regularly, about 20 minutes or until it has thickened to your desired consistency.

IF you prefer a thicker curry, dissolve the cornstarch in ½ cup warm water and stir into the chickpea curry. Serve as soon as possible after doing this as the curry will thicken more once cooled.

MEANWHILE, MAKE THE COCONUT RICE: In a large saucepan, bring the vegetable broth and coconut milk to a boil. Add the rice, cover, and cook over low heat until the liquid is fully absorbed, about 15 minutes. Remove from the heat.

FLUFF the rice with a fork and keep covered until ready to serve.

MAKE THE MANGO SALSA: In a medium bowl, stir together the mangoes, avocado, bell pepper, red onion, and cilantro. Season with salt and black pepper to taste.

PREPARE THE PLANTAINS: Line a plate with paper towels and set aside. In a deep skillet, heat 1 inch of canola oil to 375°F.

FRY the plantains in the oil until golden brown. Watch carefully, as the sugar in the plantains will caramelize quickly. Drain on the paper towels.

TRANSFER the chickpeas, rice, salsa, and plantains to a large serving dish in separate piles, sprinkle with chopped cilantro, and serve.

FAJITA TACOS

Makes 8 to 10 tacos

These tacos are a good cousin to the Backyard Quesadillas (page 80) and will pair well with the Elotes My Way (page 41) and the BBQ Tofu Bowl (page 74). While the tacos are a lighter item for your hangout menu, they come through with the flavor and will have your peoples asking for more!

2 large portobello mushrooms
1 red onion, cut into ½-inch-thick slices
1 red bell pepper, cut into ½-inch-thick strips
1 green bell pepper, cut into ½-inch-thick strips

1 teaspoon onion powder
½ teaspoon ground cumin
½ teaspoon smoked paprika
6 tablespoons vegan wine
8 to 10 almond flour tortillas
1 lime, cut into 4 wedges

CUT off the mushroom stems and use a small spoon to scrape out the black gills from the mushroom caps. Then cut the caps crosswise into ½-inch-thick strips.

IN a skillet, combine the onion and bell peppers and cook, stirring occasionally, over medium heat until tender, 3 to 5 minutes.

ADD the mushrooms, onion powder, cumin, and smoked paprika. Slowly pour in the wine and cook the mixture for 5 minutes.

SERVE the vegetable mixture with the tortillas and lime wedges for squeezing.

ENJOY!

CREAMY PESTO MAC AND CHEESE

Serves 6 to 8

For many of us, macaroni and cheese is the signature dish of someone in our family, and it makes an appearance at every holiday gathering from Thanksgiving to Kwanzaa. So how can a vegan version even compare? With pesto as an added flavoring and nondairy milk for creaminess, you'll be surprised by how well it does.

CASHEW/PESTO SAUCE:

2 cups raw cashews

2 cups unsweetened nondairy milk (such as almond, oat, coconut, etc.), plus more if needed

2 garlic cloves, peeled

⅓ cup nutritional yeast

Juice of ½ lemon

Salt and freshly ground black pepper

1 cup Basic Vegan Pesto (page 37)

PASTA AND TOPPING:

1 (16-ounce) box/bag short pasta, such as rigatoni, elbow macaroni, or penne, etc.

Softened vegan butter, for the baking dish

½ cup shredded vegan cheddar cheese

1 cup panko bread crumbs (optional)

2 tablespoons extra-virgin olive oil or melted vegan butter (optional)

Parsley, chopped, for garnish (optional)

MAKE THE CASHEW/PESTO SAUCE: Place the cashews in a bowl and water to cover. Soak for about 2 hours. Drain and rinse thoroughly. (Alternatively, if in a rush you can boil the cashews for about 20 minutes until tender.)

TRANSFER the soaked cashews to a food processor or blender. Add the milk, garlic, nutritional yeast, lemon juice, and salt and pepper to taste. Puree until very, very smooth. This could take a couple minutes depending on the strength of your processor or blender. Add the pesto and mix to combine. If the sauce is very thick, thin it with a little more milk (you can also thin it later if necessary with some of the pasta cooking water). You can make the sauce ahead and store in the fridge for 3 to 4 days or freeze.

PREPARE THE PASTA AND TOPPING: In a large pot of boiling water, cook the pasta to al dente according to the package directions. (It's always better to cook to al dente to avoid mushy pasta.) Reserve a cup or two of the pasta water before draining (this will come in handy should the cashew cream be too thick).

PREHEAT the oven to 400°F. Butter a 9-inch square baking dish.

Continued on next page

ADD the cooked pasta to the baking dish. Sprinkle in half the shredded cheddar and gently stir to combine. If you feel the cashew/pesto sauce is too thick, add some pasta water to ensure the mac and cheese doesn't dry out in the oven. I personally add ¾ to 1 cup of pasta water. Toss to combine.

TOP with the remaining cheese and sprinkle with the bread crumbs, if desired. If using bread crumbs, drizzle with the olive oil or melted butter to help with the browning.

BAKE uncovered until warmed through and golden brown on top, 15 to 20 minutes.

SERVE immediately, garnished with a sprinkling of parsley, if desired.

BASIC VEGAN PESTO

Makes 2 cups

Pesto is my favorite sauce. It's super flavorful and so easy to make. This recipe makes more than you need for the mac and cheese, so you can refrigerate any leftovers in an airtight container in the fridge for about a week, or in the freezer for up to 6 months.

2 cups fresh basil (you can keep stems on)

2 tablespoons toasted pine nuts or walnuts

2 large garlic cloves, peeled

Juice of ½ lemon

½ cup extra-virgin olive oil

Salt and freshly ground black pepper

IN a food processor, combine the basil, pine nuts, garlic, and lemon juice and process until very finely minced.

WITH the machine running, slowly drizzle in the olive oil and process until the mixture is smooth. Add salt and pepper to taste.

CUP OF KELEWELE

Serves 2

Kelewele is a traditional Jamaican snack that can be enjoyed before, during, or after your favorite drink. The bright flavors of ginger, cinnamon, paprika, and nutmeg give this island dish its potent kick.

2 ripe plantains
¼ cup fresh lemon juice
Peanut oil, for frying
½ cup whole raw or roasted cashews
7 tablespoons dark brown sugar

¼ cup diced candied ginger
1 teaspoon ground cinnamon
1 teaspoon ground nutmeg
1 teaspoon sweet paprika
Red pepper flakes, for garnish

PEEL the plantains and cut them so that they are roughly the same size of your cashews. In a bowl, toss the plantains with the lemon juice and let sit at room temperature for at least 1 hour. Drain the plantains.

IN a large frying pan, heat 2 inches of peanut oil to 400°F.

CAREFULLY add the plantains to the hot oil and fry until golden brown, 2 to 7 minutes, being careful that they don't get too brown.

MEANWHILE, in a medium bowl, combine the cashews, brown sugar, candied ginger, cinnamon, nutmeg, and paprika.

ADD the plantains and some of the oil (do NOT drain all the oil from the plantains, as they need some of the oil to melt the brown sugar) to the bowl and toss to coat with the mixture. Garnish with red pepper flakes.

SERVE while still hot and enjoy!

ELOTES MY WAY

Serves 4

My version of elotes will give you all the punch and spice of this Mexican classic but with easy vegan substitutes that will leave your taste buds and your stomach happy.

4 ears yellow or white corn, half the husks removed
2 tablespoons salt
¾ cup vegan mayonnaise
¼ cup hot sauce

½ cup grated vegan Parmesan cheese, plus more for serving
1¼ cups sliced Chinese chives
2 tablespoons vegan butter
2 teaspoons finely minced garlic

BRING a large pot of water to a boil. Add the corn and salt to the water and boil for 7 to 8 minutes.

GRILL the corn, still in half the husk, to your desired texture. Or, to cook it indoors, wrap the ears tightly in foil and place directly on burners heated to low to medium heat. Cook for 8 minutes, then open the foil carefully to check for doneness. Cook for up to 2 minutes more, if desired.

MEANWHILE, in a large bowl, mix the mayonnaise, hot sauce, Parmesan, and 1 cup of the chives until well incorporated. In a small saucepan, melt the butter and garlic together.

COAT the cooked corn with the garlic butter.

PLACE the coated corn on a serving dish and generously top it off with the mayo mixture. Add the remaining ¼ cup chives and additional cheese as desired.

GARBANZOS GUISADOS (STEWED CHICKPEAS)

Serves 6

My Abuelas Food is a Puerto Rican experience, serving food that is inspired by our grandmothers. Its mission is to serve traditional Puerto Rican cuisine that everyone is able to indulge in. Our menu provides vegan, vegetarian, and meat-based meals, plus we brew our own beer. While food brings us together, we also love to create a space filled with art, music, and community, and that is welcoming to all. We started as a pop-up in October 2018, then opened the doors of the restaurant on February 29, 2020. Our biggest accomplishment yet is having our beer distributed in our homeland, and we hope to have a brick-and-mortar location in Puerto Rico in the future.

⅓ cup extra-virgin olive oil or your preferred oil
3 tablespoons sofrito
1 tablespoon diced garlic
½ cup diced yellow onions
½ cup diced red onions
½ cup diced green onions
1 cup cubed calabaza squash, yellow squash, or potatoes
1 tablespoon dried thyme
1 tablespoon dried oregano
1 tablespoon ground cumin

1 teaspoon salt
1 teaspoon freshly ground black pepper
2 (15.5-ounce) cans chickpeas, drained and rinsed
2 cups unsalted or low-sodium vegetable broth
2 cups water
¼ cup canned tomato sauce
Handful of chopped cilantro or culantro
Cooked white rice, for serving

IN a soup pot, heat the oil over high heat. Add the sofrito and cook for a minute or so. One at a time, add the garlic, all the onions, and the squash, giving each component enough time to cook down before adding the next. This helps develop complex flavor and texture. Add the thyme, oregano, cumin, salt, and pepper and stir until fragrant.

ADD the chickpeas, broth, water, and tomato sauce. Bring to a boil and cook over medium-high heat, stirring regularly, for 30 minutes.

REDUCE the heat to medium-low, cover, and cook for 15 minutes more. Transfer to a serving plate and sprinkle with the cilantro.

SERVE with rice and enjoy!

GARLIC BUTTER TEMPEH WRAPS

Serves 4

All wraps are certainly not created equal—and this one will get you out of your wrap slump with fresh garlic, arugula, alfalfa sprouts, sun-dried tomatoes, and Key lime juice. It's perfect for a summer afternoon picnic or a formal brunch.

2 tablespoons vegan butter
2 tablespoons shaved fresh garlic
4 ounces tempeh, crumbled
Pinch of Himalayan pink salt
Pinch of freshly ground black pepper

1 cup arugula
1 cup sun-dried tomatoes, chopped
6 ounces alfalfa sprouts
2 tablespoons Key lime juice
4 large vegan tomato wraps

IN a large skillet, warm the butter over low heat until melted. Add the garlic and cook for 30 seconds.

INCREASE the heat to medium, add the tempeh, and cook for 3 to 5 minutes, agitating the pan often to prevent the tempeh from sticking. Season with the salt and pepper and remove from the heat.

IN a large bowl, toss together the arugula, sun-dried tomatoes, sprouts, and lime juice until well coated.

ADD the tempeh to the bowl and toss all the ingredients together.

DIVIDE the mixture among the wraps. For each, roll one side of the wrap over the filling, then fold in the sides and roll the rest of the wrap up like a burrito.

EAT THEM!

RUM PUNCH

Serves 4

You can't have a real Jamaican party without de rum punch! This rum punch, along with my Beet-tini (page 29), will have your guests feeling no pain and begging you for more.

2 cups pineapple juice
2 cups no-pulp orange juice
1½ cups rum
½ cup grenadine
¼ cup fresh lime juice

Ice
Lime slices, for garnish
Maraschino cherries, for garnish (optional)

IN a small pitcher, mix the pineapple juice, orange juice, rum, grenadine, and lime juice together.

POUR into ice-filled glasses and garnish with lime slices and maraschino cherries, if desired. Serve and enjoy.

HEARTY PEPPER SOUP

Serves 4 to 6

Pepper soup is known to fire up your throat and warm your belly. Make some on a cool day to help you feel some of that island heat.

3 tablespoons vegetable oil
1½ pounds plant-based ground meat substitute
3 large green bell peppers, chopped
1 large onion, chopped
¾ cup vegan red wine

3½ cups vegetable broth
2 (10.75-ounce) cans condensed tomato soup, undiluted
1 (28-ounce) can crushed tomatoes
1½ cups cooked rice
Basil leaves, for garnish (optional)

IN a deep saucepan, heat the oil over medium heat. Add the meat substitute, bell peppers, and onion and cook until the meat is no longer pink. Pour in the wine and cook until it evaporates.

STIR in the broth, tomato soup, and crushed tomatoes. Bring to a boil, then reduce the heat, cover, and simmer for at least 30 minutes, stirring occasionally.

ADD the rice and heat through.

DIVIDE the soup among serving bowls, garnish with a sprinkling of rice and a leaf or two of basil, if desired, and serve immediately.

ISLAND CAULIFLOWER PO'BOY

Serves 4

You might have thought that as a vegan you had to give up on ever again enjoying a traditional po'boy, but this cauliflower po'boy brings all the heat, the sauce, and the bite of the New Orleans classic.

CAULIFLOWER:
1 head cauliflower, cut into 1-inch florets
¼ cup plus 2 tablespoons whole wheat pastry flour
¼ cup water
¼ cup hot sauce
2 tablespoons almond butter
2 tablespoons nutritional yeast
2 teaspoons garlic powder

PO'BOY SAUCE:
½ cup vegan mayonnaise
1 tablespoon pineapple juice
1 teaspoon chopped fresh dill
1 teaspoon chopped fresh chives
1 teaspoon chopped fresh parsley
½ teaspoon garlic powder
½ teaspoon ground ginger
½ teaspoon onion powder
Salt and freshly ground black pepper

FOR ASSEMBLY:
4 vegan sub rolls
Sliced pickles (optional)
Shredded lettuce (optional)
Sliced tomato (optional)

PREHEAT the oven to 375°F.

PREPARE THE CAULIFLOWER: Place the cauliflower florets into a large bowl.

IN a medium bowl, whisk together the flour, water, hot sauce, almond butter, nutritional yeast, and garlic powder until combined. Pour the sauce mixture over the cauliflower and toss until evenly coated.

SPREAD out the florets in a single layer on a baking sheet. Bake until golden brown, about 25 minutes.

MAKE THE PO'BOY SAUCE: In a bowl, whisk together the mayonnaise, pineapple juice, dill, chives, parsley, garlic powder, ginger, and onion powder until smooth. Season with salt and pepper to taste.

TO ASSEMBLE: Place several cauliflower bites into a sub roll, bathe it with plenty of po'boy sauce, and add pickles, lettuce, and tomato, if desired.

NOW, JUMP IN THERE!

ROASTED PURPLE SWEET POTATOES

Serves 6

My purple sweet potatoes bring the funk and flavor with a fresh twist on traditional roasted potatoes by adding oyster mushrooms, fresh rosemary, and garlic.

1 pound purple sweet potatoes, peeled and cut into ½-inch cubes
½ pound oyster mushrooms, broken into individual stems
Leaves of 1 sprig fresh rosemary, finely chopped

2 tablespoons extra-virgin olive oil
2 garlic cloves, minced
Salt and freshly ground black pepper
1 shallot, roughly chopped
Basil leaves, for garnish

PREHEAT the oven to 380°F.

IN a large bowl, combine the sweet potatoes, mushrooms, rosemary, olive oil, garlic, and salt and pepper to taste, tossing to coat.

ARRANGE the sweet potato mixture on a sheet pan. Transfer to the oven and roast for 15 minutes. Stir the ingredients and add the shallot. Roast until the potatoes are fork-tender, 10 to 15 minutes more.

TRANSFER to a serving bowl, top with a few basil leaves, and enjoy fresh out of the oven!

PAELLA WITH VEGAN SHRIMP

Serves 4 to 6

Any paella is always a labor of love, but this one is worth the effort. A fresh combination of spicy flavors and vegan shrimp provides a cool alternative for your vegan friends and family.

4 ounces vegan chorizo crumbles

4 strips vegan bacon, such as Slutty Strips, chopped into ½-inch pieces

1 large onion, finely chopped

2 garlic cloves, crushed to a paste

1 fresh tomato, peeled and chopped

1 teaspoon tomato paste

1 teaspoon sweet paprika

½ cup canned crushed tomatoes

1 cup vegan dry white wine

2 cups short-grain Spanish paella rice

3 cups vegetable broth, plus 1 cup if needed

1 tablespoon onion powder

1 teaspoon garlic powder

1 teaspoon freshly cracked black pepper

½ teaspoon salt

Pinch of saffron threads

12 jumbo vegan shrimp

2 tablespoons fresh parsley, chopped, for garnish

IN a 16-inch paella pan, cook the chorizo and the bacon until the fat renders from the chorizo. Transfer the chorizo and bacon to a paper towel–lined plate and set aside. Leave the drippings in the pan.

ADD the onion to the same pan and cook over low heat, stirring often, until translucent, 3 to 5 minutes.

ADD the garlic and before it begins to brown, add the fresh tomato and stir until the liquid is evaporated. Add the tomato paste and paprika and stir well. Cook until the mixture is reduced to a jammy sauce and the oil is sizzling. Add the chorizo-bacon mixture, crushed tomatoes, and wine and simmer for 10 minutes.

ADD the rice and stir until the grains are coated in the fat. Pour in the broth, bring to a simmer, and add the onion and garlic powders, pepper, salt, and saffron. Stir well and spread the rice out evenly in the pan; do not stir again.

COOK the rice over low heat for 10 minutes, then gently tuck the shrimp into the rice. Continue cooking until the rice is tender, 8 to 10 minutes more, moving the pan and rotating it so the rice cooks evenly. Add a little more broth toward the end if the rice isn't tender yet. Gently agitate so the liquid goes to the bottom. Remove from the heat and cover to let the rice finish steaming to your desired texture.

GARNISH with parsley and serve in the pan.

PINEAPPLE RICE BOWL

Serves 4

As soon as you get this classic Thai dish under your belt, it will become part of your regular party rotation. It infuses the sweetness of the pineapple with a kick from the red pepper flakes and the nutty notes of cashew to create a perfect entrée for any casual gathering.

1 ripe pineapple, halved through the core
4 cups vegetable broth
2 cups long-grain white rice
2 Roma (plum) tomatoes, diced
6 tablespoons vegan butter

½ cup diced leeks, well cleaned
½ cup rice vinegar
1 teaspoon light brown sugar
1 tablespoon red pepper flakes
Salt and freshly ground black pepper
Green onions, chopped, for garnish

PREHEAT the broiler to high.

SET the pineapple halves rind side down and scoop out the insides, leaving a shell. Separate the core from the flesh and discard the core. Dice the pineapple flesh and set aside. Discard one half of the scooped-out shell.

SET the remaining pineapple half on a baking sheet rind side down. Broil for 3 minutes to release the sugars from the fruit. Set aside to use as the bowl.

IN a saucepan, bring the broth to a rolling boil. Add the rice, stir gently, reduce the heat to medium and cook the rice until al dente, about 15 minutes.

DRAIN the rice in a sieve (do not rinse). Transfer to a bowl and add the diced tomatoes and diced pineapple.

IN a large saucepan, melt the butter over medium heat. Add the leeks and cook until tender, about 10 minutes. Add the vinegar, brown sugar, pepper flakes, and salt and black pepper to taste. Continue cooking until the leeks are caramelized.

REMOVE from the heat and add the rice mixture to the pan, gently tossing to combine.

PLACE the pineapple/rice mixture into the broiled pineapple half for serving and garnish with the green onions.

RAW CURRY PLANTAINS

Serves 1

Due to the onset of arthritis in 2008, Tassili needed to transition to eating a 98 percent raw food diet for a year. She took courses and earned a raw food chef certification, and explored her love of spices to make her food unique and delicious. Tassili came up with a number of raw vegan dishes, such as her spicy kale, mango mushroom stew, sweet coconut corn, mango cream pie, sun and seed burger, and hot tamales. One day while daydreaming and eating her spicy kale in a wrap, she envisioned the Raw Reality Kale Wrap, soon to be introduced at her Raw Reality Eatery, Atlanta's premier vegan and raw food restaurant, in the historic West End.

3 very ripe plantains, peeled and cut into bite-size pieces
½ red bell pepper, diced
½ green bell pepper, diced
¼ red onion, diced

2 tablespoons mild curry powder
½ cup agave syrup
Pinch of salt
2 to 3 pinches cayenne pepper (optional)

IN a large bowl, combine the plantains, bell peppers, and onion and mix by hand.

ADD the curry powder and agave syrup and mix, coating the plantains. Be gentle, as the ripe plantains can easily mash. Add the salt and cayenne, if desired.

ADD LOVE and they're ready!!

SESAME BROCCOLI

Serves 2 or 3

Your everyday broccoli will take on a new attitude with this recipe. The sesame wakes up the broccoli with a mild, sweet, and nutty flavor.

1 large head broccoli, cut into florets
2 garlic cloves, minced
1 tablespoon sesame oil
2 tablespoons toasted sesame seeds

1 tablespoon Slut Dust or your favorite all-purpose seasoning blend
1 tablespoon soy sauce

IN a pot of boiling water, cook the broccoli until slightly tender, 4 to 5 minutes. Drain and rinse under cold running water to stop it from cooking.

IN a large skillet, cook the garlic in the sesame oil over low heat until the garlic sizzles.

ADD the drained broccoli, sesame seeds, and Slut Dust and toss until the broccoli is heated through.

TRANSFER to a platter, drizzle with the soy sauce, and serve immediately.

SPICY GARLIC EGGPLANT

Serves 4

If you love garlic, you will LOVE this spicy garlic dish, which is a simple blend of eggplant, red pepper flakes, black pepper, and all the garlic you can stand!

2 tablespoons extra-virgin olive oil
1 pound eggplant, unpeeled, cut into 2-inch chunks
6 dried chiles, softened in boiling water, and chopped
3 garlic cloves, thinly sliced
1 tablespoon finely minced peeled fresh ginger
¼ cup chopped green onions
2 tablespoons soy sauce, plus more if needed

1 teaspoon sugar
1 tablespoon vinegar, such as distilled white, red wine, or apple cider
¾ cup water
1 teaspoon cornstarch
1 tablespoon vegetable broth
Salt and Slut Dust (or your favorite all-purpose seasoning blend)
Mixed greens, for serving

IN a large nonstick skillet, heat 1 tablespoon of the olive oil over medium heat. Add the eggplant and cook, stirring, until browned on all sides, 1 to 2 minutes.

REMOVE the eggplant and set aside on paper towels to drain any excess oil.

ADD the remaining 1 tablespoon olive oil to the pan. Add the chiles, garlic, ginger, and green onions and cook until the green onions are soft, 45 to 60 seconds.

RETURN the eggplant to the pan and add the soy sauce, sugar, and vinegar and give it a quick toss to combine. Gradually add the water and cornstarch to the pan, then add the vegetable broth. Let the mixture simmer until the sauce is thickened and the eggplant is fork-tender.

SEASON with salt and Slut Dust, or more soy sauce if needed.

TRANSFER to a platter and serve with mixed greens.

VEGAN BOURBON CAULIFLOWER

Serves 4

Kulture Kitch'n is my vegan business that I started in 2019. At the time, I was transitioning to eating vegan, and I started Kulture Kitch'n to prove to people that we can still enjoy our favorite foods but without consuming meat and dairy. At first, Kulture Kitch'n was just a hobby: I would cook food and post pics on Instagram and Facebook and receive great feedback. I also started a YouTube channel to upload videos so people could try my recipes. After receiving an abundance of positive feedback, I decided to turn my hobby into a business. As of July 8, 2020, Kulture Kitch'n is recognized as an LLC in Maryland, and for now, it's home-based; I sell food out of my apartment on weekends. My goal is to someday own a food truck so I can tour the country, as well as ship some of my products nationwide.

BOURBON SAUCE:

1 cup water
½ cup apple juice
⅔ cup coconut aminos, liquid aminos, or soy sauce
¼ cup bourbon
2 tablespoons apple cider vinegar
¼ cup ketchup
⅔ cup packed light brown sugar
1 teaspoon minced garlic
½ teaspoon ground ginger
½ teaspoon red pepper flakes

CAULIFLOWER:

Salt
1 large head cauliflower, cut into small florets (about 4 cups)
1 teaspoon freshly ground black pepper
1 cup all-purpose flour
½ cup nondairy milk, plus more as needed
2 tablespoons cornstarch
2 teaspoons garlic powder
2 teaspoons onion powder
1 teaspoon ground cumin
1 teaspoon sweet paprika
Vegetable oil, for deep-frying

FOR SERVING:

Chopped green onions
Sesame seeds
Cooked brown rice

MAKE THE BOURBON SAUCE: In a medium saucepan, combine the water, apple juice, coconut aminos, bourbon, vinegar, ketchup, brown sugar, garlic, ground ginger, and pepper flakes. Cook over medium-low heat, stirring occasionally, until the sauce starts to thicken, about 10 minutes. Remove the bourbon sauce from the heat and set aside.

Continued on next page

PREPARE THE CAULIFLOWER: In a large pot of lightly salted boiling water, cook the cauliflower until slightly tender, 3 to 4 minutes. Drain and let cool. While cooling, season the cauliflower with 1 teaspoon salt and the black pepper.

IN a large bowl, combine the flour, ½ cup nondairy milk, the cornstarch, garlic powder, onion powder, cumin, and paprika. The consistency should be a little bit like pancake batter, so add more milk if needed.

DIP the cauliflower in the batter and arrange on a plate or tray. Once all the cauliflower has been coated, set to the side while you heat up the oil.

IN a large pot or deep fryer, heat 2 inches of oil to 350°F. Working in batches, lower the coated cauliflower into the hot oil and cook until light golden brown on both sides. Remove from the oil and place on a cooling rack. Allow to cool for 2 to 3 minutes.

TRANSFER the fried cauliflower to a large bowl and add as little or as much bourbon sauce as you want. Toss the cauliflower in the bourbon sauce until fully coated.

TO serve, garnish with green onions and sesame seeds. Serve with rice.

VEGAN FRIED FISH

Serves 2

My name is Erin Wells, aka "That Chocolate Vegan." I have always been a foodie, but after going vegan in 2016, my passion for flavors and seasoning increased. Determined to show the world that people of color could eat plant-based without sacrificing taste, I started my YouTube channel, That Chocolate Vegan, and my subscribers have been steadily growing by the thousands. In 2019, demand for my food rose beyond the screen, so I took the leap and began vending at festivals and events. Every time my clients say, "This is the best food I have had, vegan or not," my soul smiles, and that is why I love what I do.

1 large eggplant
Salt
1 tablespoon garlic powder
1 tablespoon onion powder
Roasted seaweed sheets
¼ cup Tony Chachere's Creole seasoning

3 cups (12 ounces) Zatarain's Fish-Fri seafood breading mix
2 tablespoons Old Bay seasoning
½ cup canola oil, for frying
Mustard, hot sauce, and lemon slices, for serving

CUT off the top of the eggplant, then slice lengthwise into 6 slabs (these are the "fish"). Peel off the surrounding skin.

SPRINKLE salt on both sides of the eggplant slabs and let sit for 5 minutes. Pat both sides dry.

SET up 2 oblong baking dishes for a battering station: Fill the first with enough water to cover the eggplant slices. Add the garlic powder and onion powder, and crumble at least 0.17 ounce worth of seaweed sheets into the water (you can't have too much, so no worries). Add the Creole seasoning and stir.

IN the second baking dish, mix together the Fish-Fri breading and Old Bay seasoning.

PLACE the eggplant slices into the seasoned water/seaweed mixture and let sit for at least 10 minutes to marinate.

IN a large cast-iron skillet, heat the oil over medium heat. Once the oil starts to shimmer, remove a slice of eggplant from the marinade and coat both sides in the breading mixture. Add to the skillet and cook until both sides are crisp, flipping after 2 to 3 minutes. Drain on paper towels.

REPEAT until all the slices are cooked. Serve with mustard, hot sauce, and lemon slices.

THREE
KICK UP
RUMPUS

"Kick up rumpus" in Jamaican patois means "to have a riotous good time." During the last two years of Slutty Vegan's evolution, we've had a lot to celebrate and be grateful for. In January 2019, Slutty Vegan was able to expand from our fleet of mobile food trucks to opening our first brick-and-mortar restaurant in the heart of Atlanta on Abernathy Boulevard.

The next month, we embarked on our first national tour, and less than six months later, the popularity of our first restaurant grew so wildly that we opened our second location in Jonesboro, Georgia. Then we established the Pinky Cole Foundation, dedicated to increasing generational wealth in the Black community, in September 2019.

While the COVID-19 pandemic certainly put a strain on many entrepreneurs in the food industry, we were blessed and grateful that we were able to stand strong, weather the storm, and spread the joy of vegan comfort food even further in partnerships with Rap Snacks and Shake Shack, as well as open another physical location in the Edgewood neighborhood in Southeast Atlanta.

My family and I never needed a formal reason to "kick up rumpus," whether we were cooling off on our stoops in Baltimore or enjoying the salty breezes during a much-welcome trip back home to Jamaica. In communities of color, we don't often have much individually, but through the beauty of community, our little becomes a lot. I always loved seeing groups of people come together, with one person bringing a pan of chicken and another showing up with a bowl of potato salad, and there was always that one guest who came through with the good liquor or a potent ginger beer or rum punch.

The recipes included in this chapter are some of my favorite small plates that I grew up loving as a child and a young adult, and they'll be a great addition to your own get-togethers. While the dishes featured here are a little more elevated than your standard hot dogs, burgers, and deviled eggs, they showcase the best vegan spins on classic appetizers, such as Fried Motz (page 94) and "Bacon"-Wrapped Asparagus (page 79). This chapter also includes a fresh take on fruit with Watermelon Salad (page 109) and a cool twist on a traditional egg roll, filled with a delicious avocado mix and served with a dipping sauce that includes a splash of whiskey.

These dishes celebrate the joy of small accomplishments, the power of community, and the gratitude of starting from the bottom and growing into the greatest possibilities of who you are—all good reasons to kick up rumpus.

AVOCADO EGG ROLLS

Serves 4

These egg rolls are a cool vegan spin on the classic appetizer. They get punched up with a dope dipping sauce that includes a kick of whiskey and the thick sweetness of brown sugar.

DIPPING SAUCE:

¼ cup peanut oil
½ cup yellow onion, chopped
4 Roma (plum) tomatoes, chopped
Splash of whiskey (your favorite)
½ cup packed light brown sugar
2 sprigs basil, leaves stripped and chiffonade-cut

AVOCADO ROLLS:

2 avocados, halved and pitted
4 baby bell peppers, diced
½ cup diced yellow onion
2 garlic cloves, finely minced
2 tablespoons fresh lemon juice
1 cup shredded vegan cheddar cheese
½ teaspoon Himalayan pink salt
1 teaspoon freshly cracked pink peppercorns
8 vegan egg roll wrappers
Vegetable oil, for deep-frying

MAKE THE DIPPING SAUCE: In a large skillet, heat the peanut oil over medium heat. Add the onion and cook until translucent, about 5 minutes. Add the tomatoes and cook until the tomatoes are tender, about 10 minutes.

REDUCE the heat to low and add the whiskey. (To be safe, remove the pan from the heat and pour from a portioned container.) Add the brown sugar and stir until well incorporated. Simmer until thickened to a saucy consistency.

MAKE THE AVOCADO ROLLS: Scoop the avocado flesh into a bowl. Add the bell peppers, onion, garlic, and lemon juice and mash together. Add the cheddar, salt, and pink peppercorns and fold until incorporated.

PUT a small bowl of water near your work surface. Set a wrapper on the surface with one corner facing you. Spoon ⅔ cup of the avocado mixture over the middle of the wrapper. Pull the near corner over the filling and begin rolling toward the opposite corner. Roll the wrapper halfway, then tuck the left and right sides in toward the middle. Dip your finger in the bowl of water and wet the top edge of the wrapper, then continue rolling until the wrapper is closed. Repeat until all the wrappers and avocado filling are used.

IN a large deep skillet or Dutch oven, heat 2 inches of vegetable oil to 315°F. Carefully lower the egg rolls into the oil and fry until golden brown, turning so they brown evenly on all sides, about 3 minutes per side.

STIR the basil into the dipping sauce and serve with the still-hot egg rolls.

BBQ TOFU BOWL

Serves 4

A great centerpiece for any casual gathering, this tofu bowl is filling, full of fresh flavors, and can be prepared in advance. The grilled vegetables and barbecue kick of the tofu will have your guests feeling like they're getting the best of their backyard favorites but without a meat hangover.

1 large red onion, cut into ¼-inch-thick slices

1 yellow bell pepper, cut into ¼-inch-wide strips

2 tablespoons grapeseed oil

1 (14- to 15-ounce) package extra-firm tofu, cut into 1-inch cubes

1 teaspoon extra-virgin olive oil, or more as needed

1 pineapple, peeled, cored, and cut into ½-inch-thick slices

5 ounces baby spinach

1 teaspoon coconut oil

1 cup cooked quinoa

1 cup vegan barbecue sauce

⅓ cup chopped Italian parsley

Salt and ground white pepper

PREHEAT the oven to 425°F. Line a sheet pan with parchment paper. While the oven is preheating, wrap the tofu in a clean, absorbent towel and weigh it down with a heavy object to remove excess liquid.

IN a large bowl, toss the onion and bell pepper with 1 tablespoon of the grapeseed oil. Spread the onion and bell pepper mixture on one half of the prepared sheet pan.

CUT the tofu into 2-inch cubes, toss with the remaining grapeseed oil, and place on the other half of the pan.

TRANSFER to the oven and roast the vegetables and tofu for 12 minutes. Flip the vegetables and tofu and roast until the tofu is browned, about 8 minutes more. Remove from the oven and set aside.

MEANWHILE, in a large skillet, heat the olive oil over medium-high heat. Add the pineapple slices in batches and sauté until darkly browned on both sides, adding more oil as needed, about 3 minutes on each side. Set aside on a paper towel–lined plate.

IN a medium bowl, toss the spinach with the coconut oil and squeeze by hand until wilted. Fold in the cooked quinoa.

TOSS the baked tofu with the barbecue sauce until thoroughly coated.

BUILD your tofu bowl: Make a base of the quinoa/spinach mixture, add the BBQ tofu, and top with the roasted vegetables and browned pineapples. Garnish with the parsley and season with salt and white pepper to taste.

BLACK BEAN AND PORTOBELLO TACOS

Makes 12 tacos; serves 4 to 6

Blow your friends away during your next Taco Tuesday night with these black bean and portobello tacos that pack in savory black beans, fresh mushrooms, and lots of zingy toppings.

1 pound Yukon Gold potatoes (4 to 6), peeled and cubed
1½ tablespoons extra-virgin olive oil, plus more if needed
1 canned chipotle pepper in adobo sauce, chopped, plus 1 teaspoon adobo sauce
1 tablespoon chili powder
½ teaspoon ground cumin

Coarse salt and freshly ground black pepper
4 portobello mushrooms, sliced
1 large yellow onion, sliced
12 corn tortillas
¼ cup sliced radishes
¼ cup chopped tomatoes
¼ cup chopped fresh cilantro
½ cup salsa

PREHEAT the oven to 400°F.

ON a large sheet pan, arrange the potatoes and drizzle with ½ tablespoon of the olive oil and toss to coat. Bake the potatoes for 30 minutes, stirring once or twice.

MEANWHILE, in a small bowl, stir together the remaining 1 tablespoon olive oil, the chipotle pepper, adobo sauce, chili powder, and cumin, and season with salt and black pepper to taste.

WHEN the potatoes have baked for 30 minutes, add the mushrooms and onion to the pan and drizzle everything with the chipotle mixture. Stir to coat and add an extra drizzle of olive oil if needed.

RETURN the pan to the oven and continue to bake until the potatoes are fork-tender, about another 20 minutes, stirring once.

MEANWHILE, in a large skillet, heat a few drops of oil over medium heat. Working in batches, add however many corn tortillas you can fit in a single layer and cook about 1 minute on each side until softened and lightly charred.

SERVE the taco filling in the charred tortillas. Top with the sliced radishes, tomatoes, cilantro, and salsa.

"BACON" BROCCOLI SLAW

Serves 2 or 3

Get ready to take in the compliments when you make this slammin' side dish. This broccoli slaw takes traditional coleslaw up a notch and pulls in the new and unexpected flavors of jalapeños, Roma tomatoes, edamame, and sesame seeds, and uses tempeh to stand in for the bacon.

2 tablespoons coconut oil
½ cup crumbled tempeh
½ cup rice vinegar
Juice of 1 lime
7 tablespoons light brown sugar
Pinch of salt
2 jalapeños, seeded and sliced
2 Roma (plum) tomatoes, julienned
2 cups shredded broccoli stems
1 cup shredded carrots

½ yellow onion, sliced
½ red onion, sliced
½ cup shredded red cabbage
6 ounces shelled fresh edamame
1 tablespoon sesame seeds
4 sprigs fresh cilantro, for garnish
½ cup bean sprouts, for garnish (optional)
Vegan ranch dressing and hot sauce, for serving

IN a medium skillet, heat the coconut oil over medium heat. Add the tempeh and cook until browned and crispy, about 8 minutes. Remove from the heat and set aside to cool.

IN a large bowl, combine the vinegar, lime juice, and brown sugar. Whisk until the brown sugar is dissolved. Whisk in the salt.

ADD the jalapeños, tomatoes, broccoli, carrots, both onions, the cabbage, edamame, and sesame seeds in a bowl. Toss until thoroughly mixed together.

REFRIGERATE for at least 30 minutes to blend the flavors. Transfer to a serving dish and garnish with the cilantro and bean sprouts, if using.

SERVE with ranch dressing and hot sauce on the side.

"BACON"-WRAPPED ASPARAGUS

Serves 2

You might have thought you had to leave behind your favorite bacon-wrapped recipes, but with my Slutty Strips, all those classics will have a fresh, new life. These "bacon"-wrapped asparagus can be baked in the oven.

1 red bell pepper, sliced
Extra-virgin olive oil
Salt
7 spears asparagus, ends trimmed
7 Slutty Strips, or vegan bacon of choice
½ teaspoon freshly cracked black pepper

½ teaspoon dried oregano
1 teaspoon fresh lemon juice
½ teaspoon grated lemon zest, for garnish
Lemon slices, for garnish

PREHEAT the oven to 400°F.

IN a medium bowl, toss the bell pepper slices with a little olive oil. Spread on a sheet pan and roast until tender, 10 to 12 minutes. Remove from the oven and set aside, but leave the oven on.

MEANWHILE, set up a large bowl of ice and water. In a medium pot of boiling salted water, blanch the asparagus for 30 seconds. Carefully remove the asparagus from the hot water and transfer to the ice bath to cool, about 30 seconds. Pat dry with a kitchen towel and drizzle with 2 tablespoons olive oil.

WRAP each spear of asparagus with a Slutty Strip and place on a clean sheet pan. Season with the cracked black pepper, oregano, and 1½ teaspoons salt.

TRANSFER to the oven and roast until the asparagus is tender, about 7 minutes.

REMOVE the asparagus from the oven and place it on a serving dish. Drizzle with the lemon juice and garnish with the lemon zest, roasted red pepper, and lemon slices.

SERVE immediately.

BACKYARD QUESADILLAS

Makes 16 quesadillas

These quesadillas are a surefire party starter. They are super easy, light, and so good that your party guests will have no idea that they're chowing down on a meatless version of the Mexican classic.

1 tablespoon extra-virgin olive oil
1 large sweet potato, peeled and cut into ½-inch cubes
1 cup canned vegetarian refried beans
1 cup canned black beans, drained and rinsed
1 cup Pineapple Salsa (page 169)

1 cup fresh arugula
¼ teaspoon onion powder
¼ teaspoon garlic powder
¼ teaspoon chili powder
¼ teaspoon ground cumin
32 whole wheat tortillas (6- to 8-inch-diameter)

PREHEAT the oven to 350°F. Coat a baking sheet with the olive oil.

ARRANGE the sweet potato on the baking sheet and bake until tender to the poke, about 40 minutes.

IN a large bowl, combine the sweet potatoes, refried beans, black beans, salsa, and arugula. Fold in the onion powder, garlic powder, chili powder, and cumin.

MAKING one quesadilla at a time, heat a large skillet over medium to medium-high heat. Add a tortilla to the pan. Top the tortilla with about ⅓ cup of the quesadilla mixture. Place a second tortilla on top of the quesadilla mixture and cook until the bottom tortilla is golden brown. Flip the quesadilla and brown the other side.

REPEAT until all the mixture and tortillas are used. Cut the quesadillas into wedges and EAT!

REFRIED BEAN AND PORTOBELLO SOFT TACOS

Serves 4

Many home cooks think that cooking vegan should only be attempted with dishes from your own culture. Not so! Feel free to give Mexican, Italian, and Chinese recipes a try, even when you're just starting out. You'll discover lots of dishes you love, like these soft tacos that are better than the ones you get from your favorite takeout spot!

TACO FILLING:

2 extra-large portobello mushrooms, cut into ½-inch-thick slices

1 red bell pepper, cut into ½-inch-thick strips

½ red onion, cut into ½-inch-thick rings or half moons (optional)

2 tablespoons canned chipotle peppers in adobo sauce

1 tablespoon grapeseed oil

1 tablespoon chili powder

1 teaspoon ground coriander

1 teaspoon ground cumin

1 teaspoon salt

SOFT TACOS:

1 (15- to 16-ounce) can vegetarian refried black beans

4 (8-inch) whole wheat tortillas

FOR SERVING:

Diced avocado

Lime slices

Diced red onion

Chopped cilantro

MAKE THE TACO FILLING: Preheat the oven to 425°F. Line a sheet pan with parchment paper.

ARRANGE the mushrooms, bell pepper, and onion, if desired, in separate areas on the prepared sheet pan.

IN a small bowl, mix together the chipotle peppers, grapeseed oil, chili powder, coriander, and cumin.

BRUSH both sides of mushrooms liberally with the chipotle mixture, then use the remaining mixture to lightly brush the bell pepper and onion. Sprinkle the portobellos with the salt.

TRANSFER to the oven and roast until the portobellos are fork-tender, about 20 minutes.

MEANWHILE, FOR THE TACOS: In a medium saucepan, heat the refried beans.

IN a large skillet, heat the tortillas. Spread each tortilla with some refried black beans and, dividing evenly, top with the chipotle portobellos, bell pepper, and onion. Serve with the garnishes on the side.

BLACK PEA BURGERS

Serves 4

These black pea burgers are one of my favorite recipes for surprising the most die-hard meat lovers with how flavorful, moist, and delicious a good plant-based burger can be. With the right blend of cayenne pepper, 4 whole garlic cloves, and good kicks of red bell pepper and red onions, my black pea burger comes out the gate swinging with flavor and hearty texture that will take your party to a whole other level.

1 (15-ounce) can black-eyed peas, drained and rinsed
1 cup cornmeal
½ cup fresh corn kernels
½ cup diced red bell pepper
½ cup diced red onion
1 green onion, white and green parts, chopped
4 garlic cloves, chopped
2 ounces chives, minced
1 tablespoon vegan Worcestershire sauce
4 teaspoons paprika
2 tablespoons cayenne pepper
1 teaspoon dried thyme
½ teaspoon salt
½ teaspoon freshly ground black pepper
All-purpose flour, as needed
Canola oil, for frying
4 vegan buns
Chipotle Vegenaise or your favorite burger condiment
Lettuce (optional)
Sliced tomato (optional)
Sliced red onion (optional)

IN a food processor, combine the black-eyed peas, cornmeal, corn, bell pepper, red onion, green onion, garlic, chives, Worcestershire sauce, paprika, cayenne pepper, thyme, salt, and black pepper and pulse until the ingredients are finely chopped and well mixed, stopping to scrape down the sides of the bowl as needed. Test the mixture by forming into a patty to see if it holds shape; if it doesn't, add all-purpose flour, a little at a time, until it does. Form the mixture into four 1-inch-thick patties.

COAT the bottom of a large skillet with oil and set it over medium heat until the oil starts to shimmer. Add the patties 2 or 3 at a time to avoid overcrowding the skillet. Cook until lightly browned and crisp, about 5 minutes on each side. Set aside on a paper towel–lined plate to drain.

SERVE the patties on the buns with Vegenaise and, if desired, lettuce, tomato, and/or red onion.

EAT them thangs!

CHEESY BERRY POPPERS

Serves 4

These poppers are a smoother take on a jalapeño popper with a fruity pop of blueberry preserves and vegan bacon, such as my signature Slutty Strips.

2 tablespoons extra-virgin olive oil
2 Slutty Strips, or vegan bacon of choice
¼ cup sunflower oil
8 to 10 mini bell peppers, halved through the stem and seeded

¼ teaspoon salt
4 ounces vegan cream cheese
2 generous tablespoons blueberry preserves (no high fructose corn syrup)

IN a large skillet, heat the olive oil over medium heat. Add the bacon and move it around in the pan to prevent sticking. Cook until slightly browned, about 2 minutes on each side. Remove the strips from the pan, allow them to cool, and hand tear them into bite-size pieces. Set aside.

IN the same pan, heat the sunflower oil over low heat. Add the bell peppers skin-side down, sprinkle with the salt, and sauté for 2 minutes to sear the bell peppers' skin. Remove from the heat and set aside.

IN a small bowl, mix the cream cheese and blueberry preserves together.

DIVIDING evenly, spoon the cream cheese mixture into the bell pepper halves. Top with the bacon pieces. Enjoy immediately as a snack!

CHIPOTLE-STUFFED AVOCADOES

Serves 4

Crystal Shae is a woman of many talents and experiences. She is a coach, nutrition thought leader, and, most important, one of Atlanta's OG raw vegan chefs, among a host of other things.

Crystal Shae has experienced no shortage of ups and downs throughout her life, so she understands what it means to have your life change, for the better and for the worse. Switching to a raw vegan diet changed the way she felt on a daily basis, but it wasn't just the de-bloating, better skin, more restful sleep, and weight loss; Crystal also felt a profound change on a spiritual level.

Health is so much more than how you look and how you feel. Health is a true state of being, and Crystal Shae wants to help more people get there through food, flavor, and guidance. She knows that when people decide to make different choices, even if they're small one, their lives will begin to change before their eyes.

VEGETABLE FILLING:
1 cup peeled and diced jicama
1 teaspoon minced fresh sage
3 celery stalks, chopped
1 cup diced tomatoes
1 cup hulled pumpkin seeds
½ cup diced onion
1 teaspoon salt

DRESSING:
1 cup raw cashews, soaked for
  2 to 3 hours and drained
2 tablespoons extra-virgin olive oil
¼ cup fresh lemon juice
1 garlic clove, peeled
1 chipotle pepper in adobo sauce
¼ cup water

ASSEMBLY:
4 avocadoes, halved and pitted
Unshelled pumpkin seeds (optional)
Crushed black pepper

MAKE THE VEGETABLE FILLING: In a bowl, combine the jicama, sage, celery, tomatoes, hulled pumpkin seeds, onion, and salt.

MAKE THE DRESSING: In a high-powered blender, combine the cashews, olive oil, lemon juice, garlic, chipotle pepper, and water. Blend until smooth.

ADD the dressing to the vegetables and toss until combined, garnish with unshelled pumpkin seeds, if desired, and sprinkle with crushed black pepper.

DIVIDING evenly, spoon the filling into the avocado halves and serve immediately.

DEVILED N'EGG

Serves 4

If you love oldie-but-goodie stuffed-food favorites like Crystal Shae's stuffed avocados on page 88, then you definitely need to try this vegan version of the comfort classic deviled eggs.

MAYO:

1 cup raw cashews, soaked for 2 to 3 hours and drained
¼ cup fresh lemon juice
¼ cup water, plus more as needed for blending
1 tablespoon agave syrup
1 tablespoon ground turmeric
1 tablespoon ground cumin
1 tablespoon mustard powder
1 teaspoon black salt (kala namak)
1 teaspoon ground thyme

VEGETABLES:

6 to 8 Roma (plum) tomatoes
1 teaspoon black salt (kala namak)
½ cup finely chopped celery
½ cup finely chopped red bell pepper
½ cup finely diced red onion

FOR GARNISH:

Sweet paprika
Fresh thyme
Green onions, chopped

MAKE THE MAYO: In a high-powered blender, combine the cashews, lemon juice, water, agave syrup, turmeric, cumin, mustard powder, black salt, and thyme. Blend until smooth, adding more water if needed.

PREPARE THE VEGETABLES: Slice the tomatoes in half. Remove the tomato flesh with a melon baller (discard the flesh). Sprinkle the tomato shells with the black salt and turn them upside down on a paper towel to drain.

IN a small bowl, combine the celery, bell pepper, and onion. Mix by hand until combined. Add the mayo mixture to the vegetables and stir until completely coated.

FILL the tomato shells with the vegetables and garnish with paprika, fresh thyme, and green onions.

EGGPLANT FRIES

Serves 2

I'll bet you had no idea that I could flip eggplant into becoming your next favorite fry. With just a little patience while cutting your eggplant into lengthwise strips and then adding a little more love when you fry them, these eggplant fries are sure to give your ordinary fries a run for their money.

1 eggplant
½ cup chickpea flour
1 teaspoon cornstarch
1 teaspoon dried basil
1 teaspoon dried oregano
1 teaspoon sweet paprika
1 teaspoon Slut Dust, or your favorite all-purpose seasoning blend
2 tablespoons ground flaxseed

6 tablespoons water
1½ cups unsweetened almond milk
1½ cups gluten-free bread crumbs
¼ cup nutritional yeast (or grated vegan Parmesan)
Salt and freshly ground black pepper
Canola oil, for frying
Store-bought marinara sauce, for serving

CUT the eggplant into large french fry shapes. The easiest way to do this is to cut the ends off the eggplant, peel it, then stand it up. Slice the eggplant lengthwise into ½-inch-thick slabs. Then lay each slab down and cut it lengthwise into ½-inch-wide sticks. If you want your fries long, leave them like this. If you want them shorter, cut those sticks in half.

IN a shallow dish, mix together the chickpea flour, cornstarch, basil, oregano, paprika, and Slut Dust.

IN a second shallow bowl, mix the ground flaxseed and water into a loose paste. Stir in the almond milk.

IN a third shallow bowl, mix together the bread crumbs and nutritional yeast (or grated Parm). Season with salt and pepper to taste.

LINE a plate with paper towels. In a deep pan or skillet, heat about 2 inches of oil until it begins to shimmer.

TOSS the eggplant in the chickpea flour mixture, then dip in the milk/flax mixture, then into the bread crumbs.

FRY the eggplant until golden brown, 2 to 3 minutes on each side.

TRANSFER to the paper towels to drain. Serve with marinara sauce. Enjoy!

FRIED MOTZ

Serves 4

You won't believe you're not eating real mozzarella cheese after you get a hold of this recipe! With vegan mozzarella as an easy swap-in, you will never have to miss out on this appetizer again.

¾ cup all-purpose flour
½ teaspoon dried oregano
½ teaspoon sweet paprika
½ teaspoon salt
½ teaspoon freshly ground black
  pepper
½ cup egg substitute

1 cup vegan bread crumbs
Canola oil, for frying
10 ounces vegan mozzarella cheese,
  cut into 2-inch cubes
Your favorite dipping sauce, for
  serving

SET up a dredging station: In one shallow bowl, mix together the flour, oregano, paprika, salt, and pepper. Place the egg substitute in a second bowl. Place the bread crumbs in the third bowl.

IN a deep pan, pour in the oil until it reaches halfway up the side of the pan and heat over medium-high heat.

ROLL the mozzarella cubes in the flour mixture, then gently place them in the egg substitute, and finally coat them with the bread crumbs.

WORKING in batches, carefully drop the mozzarella cubes into the hot oil and cook until golden brown, about 3 minutes.

REMOVE from the oil and drain on a paper towel–lined plate.

SERVE with your favorite dipping sauce.

HABANERO MARGARITAS

Makes 2 cocktails

If you like that heat, this cocktail—which infuses your favorite tequila with habanero—will put that fire on your lips.

1 ripe mango, pitted and cubed
1 habanero pepper, seeded and sliced
1 cup orange juice
Juice of 2 small limes
2½ to 3 ounces silver tequila, to taste

1 to 3 tablespoons agave syrup or maple syrup, to taste
1 teaspoon chili powder
¼ teaspoon sea salt
Lime wedges, for rimming

IN a blender, combine the mango, half of the habanero slices, the orange juice, lime juice, tequila, and agave syrup and blend until creamy and smooth. Taste and adjust the sweetness and the amount of alcohol as desired.

TO serve chilled, either blend in a large handful of ice cubes to make a frozen margarita or, working in two batches, transfer the mixture to a cocktail shaker with plenty of ice and shake vigorously.

ON a small plate, mix together the chili powder and sea salt. Wet the rims of two serving glasses with a lime wedge and immediately dip in the salt/chili powder mixture (or substitute just salt or sugar). Pour the margarita into the glasses and garnish with habanero slices.

VEGAN KING "SCALLOPS"

Serves 2

Culinary Groove is a combination of great food accompanied by great music. It was inspired by the vision of bringing people together to rejoice over those two common factors that we all enjoy.

Born and raised in Atlanta, I create a variety of delicious creative entrées to groove the soul. I started the business in 2018 to fulfill a dream of getting people to try different food ideas, and I see Culinary Groove constantly growing until it becomes a household name.

2 king oyster (aka king trumpet) mushrooms
1 tablespoon garlic powder
1 tablespoon Old Bay seasoning
1 teaspoon salt
1 tablespoon extra-virgin olive oil
½ tablespoon vegan butter

1 (14.5-ounce) can diced tomatoes
½ cup sliced white onions
1 tablespoon vegetarian oyster sauce
1 tablespoon light brown sugar
1 teaspoon minced fresh parsley, plus more for garnish

CUT 1-inch-thick rounds from the mushroom stems (the size of scallops) and score a checkerboard pattern on the bottom and top of the rounds, if desired.

SLICE the mushroom caps and set aside. Season the mushroom "scallops" with the garlic powder, Old Bay, and salt.

IN a large skillet, heat the olive oil over medium heat. Place the mushroom "scallops" in the pan and brown each side until golden brown, about 5 minutes. Once each side is seared, remove the "scallops" from the pan.

ADD the butter to the pan. Then add the reserved sliced mushrooms, diced tomatoes, diced onions, vegetarian oyster sauce, brown sugar, and parsley. Sauté for 10 minutes and that's it.

DIVIDE the mushroom/tomato mixture between two plates, top with the mushroom "scallops," and garnish with parsley.

MIDNIGHT TODDY

Makes 2 toddies

When you feel the beginning of a cold coming down on you, the Midnight Toddy can help you curb that ick with a warming blend of agave syrup, cinnamon, nutmeg, and, if you want to punch it up a notch, a good splash of your favorite whiskey.

16 ounces water
2 bags spiced tea
2 cinnamon sticks
2 lemon wedges
2 pinches of grated nutmeg

1 ounce agave syrup
2 teaspoons fresh lemon juice
4 ounces whiskey (optional)
2 lemon slices, for garnish

IN a small saucepan, bring the water to a boil. Add the tea bags, remove the pan from the heat, and let steep for about 5 minutes, or to your desired strength.

POUR the tea into two mugs.

TO each mug add 1 cinnamon stick, 1 lemon wedge, a pinch of nutmeg, and half the agave syrup, lemon juice, and whiskey, if desired. Garnish each with a slice of lemon and enjoy while warm!

VEGAN CHEESESTEAK EGG ROLLS

Makes 4 egg rolls

Egg rolls are the ultimate appetizer munchie. And swapping out for meat- and dairy-free items doesn't take away any of the flavor in a single juicy bite.

4 (7-inch) egg roll wrappers
2 slices vegan provolone cheese, halved
2 slices vegan white or yellow American cheese, halved
12 ounces vegan beef
Vegetable oil, for deep-frying

SET an egg roll wrapper with a corner facing you, like a diamond. Wet the top two edges of the wrapper with water. Place a half-slice each of provolone and American cheese in the center of the wrapper. Place a quarter of the vegan beef on top.

FOLD the two side corners in, pull up the bottom to slightly form an envelope, then roll it up. Continue constructing the egg rolls until all the wrappers, cheese, and vegan beef have been used. Set aside.

IN a large frying pan, heat 2 inches of oil over medium heat until it shimmers. Add the egg rolls to the hot oil and fry until browned on all sides, about 5 minutes. Serve hot.

VEGAN POTATO SALAD

Serves 10-plus

Yusef El-Amin was once a frozen-fish distributor. Then one day the freezer broke and he had two choices: throw out all the fish or use it. After frying up the thawed-out fish and inviting the community to the now legendary "Friday Fish Fry," the public wanted more! Soon after, Chef El-Amin and his siblings launched a brick-and-mortar soul food restaurant in New Rochelle, New York. Now they are excited to bring their freshly prepared prepackaged vegan sides and entrées to the market as a healthier alternative to traditional soul food that doesn't compromise taste.

Note: This is a very large recipe. Feel free to scale it down.

20 pounds potatoes, peeled, diced, and boiled until fork-tender
1 tablespoon Himalayan pink salt
2 tablespoons coarsely ground black pepper
3 tablespoons granulated onion
1 cup relish
2 tablespoons yellow mustard
4 cups vegan mayonnaise
¼ cup agave syrup
Paprika, for garnish
Chopped chives, for garnish

IN a large bowl, combine the potatoes with the salt, pepper, and granulated onion.

TOP the potatoes with ingredients in this order: the relish, mustard, mayo, and agave syrup.

WITH open hands, gently mix together. (DO NOT SQUEEZE THE INGREDIENTS!)

PLACE the potato salad onto a large serving platter and sprinkle with paprika and chives for garnish. Serve immediately.

VEGAN FRIED RICE

Serves 2

You don't have to sacrifice one ounce of flavor with this vegan fried rice, which is packed with sesame oil, carrots, peas, green onions, and firm tofu.

12 ounces extra-firm tofu

1 cup long- or short-grain brown rice, well rinsed

4 tablespoons tamari

2 or 3 tablespoons organic brown sugar, to taste

1 tablespoon peanut butter

4 teaspoons minced garlic

2 teaspoons chili-garlic sauce, plus more for serving

1 teaspoon sesame oil

1 cup chopped green onions

½ cup green peas

½ cup diced carrots

PREHEAT the oven to 400°F. Line a baking sheet with parchment paper. While the oven is preheating, wrap the tofu in a clean, absorbent towel and weigh it down with a heavy object to remove excess liquid.

CUT the tofu into ½-inch cubes and arrange on the prepared baking sheet. Bake for about 30 minutes or until firm and golden. Set aside.

IN a large pot, bring 1 cup water to a boil. Once boiling, stir in the rice. Boil on high, uncovered, for 30 minutes. Drain in a sieve and return to the pot. Cover with a lid and let steam for 10 minutes.

IN a small bowl, whisk together 3 tablespoons of the tamari, the brown sugar, peanut butter, 2 teaspoons of the garlic, the chili-garlic sauce, and sesame oil.

ONCE the tofu is done baking, add it to the sauce and marinate for 5 minutes, stirring occasionally.

HEAT a cast-iron skillet over medium heat. Once hot, scoop the tofu into the pan, leaving most of the sauce behind. Cook for 3 to 4 minutes, stirring occasionally, until deep golden brown on all sides. Reduce the heat if it is browning too quickly. Remove from the pan and set aside.

TO the hot pan, add the remaining 2 teaspoons garlic, the green onions, peas, and carrots. Sauté for 3 to 4 minutes, stirring occasionally, and season with the remaining 1 tablespoon tamari.

ADD the cooked rice, tofu, and remaining sauce and stir. Cook over medium-high heat for 3 to 4 minutes, stirring frequently. Serve immediately with extra chili-garlic sauce on the side.

WATERMELON SALAD

Serves 1

A cool, easy-to-make side dish, watermelon salad is perfect for a midsummer night joint and will leave you satisfied with nice pops of cashew cheese, watercress, and fresh pressed mango juice.

6 ounces watercress
2 cups cubed seeded watermelon
4 ounces cashew cheese crumbles
½ cup freshly pressed mango juice

¼ cup coconut milk
2 tablespoons grapeseed oil
1 teaspoon sesame seeds

ARRANGE the watercress on a large plate. Top with the watermelon. Crumble and sprinkle the cashew cheese on top of the watermelon.

IN a small bowl, whisk together the mango juice and coconut milk. Slowly add the grapeseed oil, whisking rapidly until the mixture is emulsified.

DRIZZLE the dressing over the salad. Garnish with the sesame seeds and serve.

FOUR
GOOD OL'
SOUTHERN
COMFORT

When customers walk into a Slutty Vegan restaurant, they are always greeted with a joyful welcome, some "slutty" humor, and vivid colors. I designed the brand to evoke a feeling of pleasure and curiosity. I want people to feel excited when they visit Slutty Vegan, to share the experience with their friends and loved ones, and to be eager to return. Most people are not aware of this, but Slutty Vegan has never had to pay for marketing. The secret to our brand's success is that we put the customer experience in the center of every business decision. How do people feel when they eat good food . . . when they gather?

The energy in the Slutty Vegan restaurants feels like home to me. My Jamaican heritage has taught me a lot when it comes to gathering and celebrating culture, and community. But even beyond this, my parents raised me and my siblings to eat from the land—I grew up mostly vegetarian. Both of my parents are lifelong Rastafari, members of a religious and social movement developed in Jamaica in the 1930s. While most may think of Rastafarians wearing their hair long and locked, there is so much more to their culture. For example, Rastafarians usually dress in colors of red, green, gold, and black (which symbolize the life force of blood, herbs, royalty, and African heritage).

The Slutty Vegan restaurants are adorned in similar hues of red, black, and gold. When a customer steps into one of the restaurants, there is always lively music, which reminds me of reggae music—another hallmark of the Rastafari movement, made most popular by Bob Marley. While I am not a practicing Rastafari, spiritually I believe in leading with empathy and love in all things, just like they do. I want people to feel good when they visit my restaurants.

I remember cooking with my grandmother when I was a young child and always having a home filled with extended family and neighbors. There was joy in the air and love around me. Community gatherings are so much a part of who I am that even when I was a teen I was throwing my own block parties. I laugh sometimes because even though I didn't always serve food, the parties would always sell out because they involved music and good vibes.

Much of what people feel when they visit a Slutty Vegan restaurant is the environment I have always known. The grand opening of the first location, on Ralph David Abernathy Boulevard in Southwest Atlanta, was essentially a block party! This energy made me nostalgic and so proud. Customers were happy, and there was good music, giveaways, social media conversations, and, of course, great food.

Only those in my personal network know this, but I started my own vegan journey more than a decade ago. I was looking for a change and wanted to feel more in alignment with myself. I was working in television production and had a deep yearning to step back into the entrepreneurial world. However, what I most yearned for was community, so I launched a vegan Facebook group in 2014, and it exploded with popularity. Most of the members were simply curious about how to pivot to a vegan lifestyle while still enjoying their favorite cultural foods. Engaging with the group members—a virtual gathering of sorts—solidified for me that there was a market in the vegan industry for an unapologetically Black cultural brand.

When I walk into the Slutty Vegan restaurants or meet customers during our food truck tours, it feels like I've come full circle—people gathering to enjoy food created with my cultural values and roots in mind. Often, they are trying vegan food for the first time, and like when I opened my first restaurant, I feel nostalgic and proud.

AMAZING MAC 'N' CHEEZ

Serves 6

If it's been a while since you've enjoyed good mac 'n' cheese, this amazing version will give you the same ooey gooey goodness by swapping in your favorite vegan cheese, nutritional yeast, and coconut milk.

CHEESE SAUCE:
½ cup vegan butter, plus more for the baking dish
6 tablespoons all-purpose flour
3 (13.5-ounce) cans unsweetened coconut milk
1 cup vegetable broth
8 ounces vegan cheddar cheese, shredded
3 tablespoons Dijon mustard
1 cup nutritional yeast
2 tablespoons onion powder
2 tablespoons garlic powder
2 teaspoons smoked paprika
1 teaspoon salt
1 teaspoon freshly ground black pepper

FOR THE CASSEROLE:
16 ounces elbow macaroni
2 cups bread crumbs or panko
2 tablespoons vegan butter, melted

Chopped parsley, for garnish

MAKE THE CHEESE SAUCE: In a large saucepan, melt the butter. Add the flour and stir well. Pour in the coconut milk and vegetable broth and whisk to smooth out the lumps. Add the cheese and whisk until the mixture starts to boil, then keep whisking until it thickens.

REMOVE it from the heat and whisk in the mustard, nutritional yeast, onion powder, garlic powder, smoked paprika, salt, and pepper.

FOR THE CASSEROLE: Preheat the oven to 400°F. Butter a 9 × 13-inch baking dish and set aside.

IN a large pot of boiling water, cook the macaroni according to the package directions. Drain, rinse, and return to the pot. Add the sauce to the pasta and stir to coat. Transfer to the prepared baking dish and smooth the top.

IN a medium bowl, stir together the bread crumbs and melted butter and toss to evenly moisten the crumbs. Sprinkle evenly over the the macaroni and cheese.

BAKE until the topping is golden brown, about 20 minutes. Serve garnished with chopped parsley.

BARBECUED "BEEF" LOAF

Serves 4

Where's the beef? Not in this recipe—but your friends and family will surely think this vegan "beef" loaf is the real thing, as it is infused with garlic and liquid smoke and can be served to perfection with my Garlic Herb Mashed Potatoes (page 118).

1 to 2 tablespoons grapeseed oil
1 cup diced onions
1 cup diced carrots
2 cups diced celery
3 garlic cloves, minced
2 (15-ounce) cans chickpeas, drained and rinsed
2 cups bread crumbs

2 tablespoons ground flaxseed
2 tablespoons nutritional yeast
2 tablespoons tamari
2 tablespoons vegan Worcestershire sauce, plus 1 teaspoon
¼ cup ketchup, plus ⅓ cup
1 teaspoon liquid smoke
Chopped chives, for garnish (optional)

PREHEAT the oven to 400°F. Line the bottom of a 9 × 5-inch loaf pan with parchment paper.

IN a large skillet, heat the oil over medium heat. Add the onions, carrots, celery, and garlic and sauté until the onions are translucent, 3 to 5 minutes. Remove from the heat and set aside.

IN a large bowl, mash the chickpeas with a fork. You do not want them to be completely pasty or mushy. Add the cooked veggies, bread crumbs, ground flaxseed, nutritional yeast, tamari, the 2 tablespoons Worcestershire sauce, the ¼ cup ketchup, and the liquid smoke. Stir with a large spoon until very well combined.

PRESS the loaf mixture into the prepared pan, pushing down evenly with your hand. Cover with foil and bake for 30 minutes.

MEANWHILE, in a small bowl, stir together the remaining 1 teaspoon Worcestershire sauce and ⅓ cup ketchup.

REMOVE the foil, spread the ketchup topping evenly on top of the loaf, and bake uncovered for another 15 minutes. Remove from the oven.

ALLOW the loaf to sit for at least 15 minutes before slicing if you can; it will hold up better.

SERVE garnished with chopped chives, if desired.

GARLIC HERB MASHED POTATOES

Serves 4

There's nothing more warm and toasty than mashed potatoes, especially when it's made creamy and smooth with vegan butter and a couple of dairy-free milks for layered flavor.

8 Yukon Gold potatoes, peeled and chopped
1 cup unsweetened almond milk
¼ cup vegan cream or coconut milk
4 ounces vegan butter, cut into pieces, plus more for serving
5 sprigs fresh thyme

2 tablespoons chopped fresh sage
4 garlic cloves, minced
1 teaspoon garlic powder
2 teaspoons Himalayan pink salt
¼ cup chopped fresh parsley
Freshly ground black pepper

BRING a large pot of water to a boil. Add the potatoes and cook until completely soft, about 20 minutes. Drain and transfer to a large bowl.

IN a small saucepan, combine the almond milk, cream, butter, thyme, sage, garlic, garlic powder, and salt. Bring to a simmer and cook for about 10 minutes. Remove from the heat.

STRAIN the mixture through a sieve into the bowl of potatoes and mix until the potatoes are smooth and creamy.

TRANSFER to a serving bowl. Top with butter, the chopped parsley, and black pepper.

HOME-FRIED POTATOES WITH "EGGS"

Serves 2 or 3

Don't let anyone tell you that vegan dishes can't be full of protein! This warm and hearty dish is perfect for one of those breakfast-for-dinner meals.

5 red potatoes, scrubbed and cut into quarters
¼ teaspoon Cajun seasoning
¼ teaspoon garlic-pepper seasoning
½ teaspoon salt
¼ teaspoon freshly ground black pepper
Sunflower oil or extra-virgin olive oil, for pan-frying

½ bell pepper, any color, diced
½ medium onion, diced
2 cloves garlic, minced
2 vegan sausage links, cut into 1-inch rounds
1 cup grape tomatoes
½ cup fresh spinach
½ cup Just Egg

PREHEAT the oven to 375°F.

ARRANGE the potatoes on a large sheet pan. Season with the Cajun seasoning, garlic-pepper seasoning, salt, and black pepper.

ROAST until tender, about 20 minutes. Remove the sheet pan from the oven, but leave the oven on.

MEANWHILE, in a large skillet, heat 1 tablespoon oil over medium heat. Add the bell pepper, onion, and garlic and sauté for 5 minutes. Add the vegan sausage and cook until the sausage is browned, about 10 minutes. Add the tomatoes and spinach and sauté for 5 minutes.

ADD the sautéed vegetables and sausage to the sheet pan with the potatoes and return everything to the oven and continue cooking until the potatoes are fork-tender, about 20 minutes.

IN a clean large skillet, heat 2 tablespoons oil. Add half of the Just Egg and fry until it begins to bubble along the edges. Add the remaining Just Egg, fry both portions to the desired doneness, and remove from the heat.

STIR together the potatoes, roasted veggies, and sausage and transfer to a large serving dish. Top with the Just Egg and serve immediately.

BLACK-EYED PEA STEW

Serves 4 to 6

If you're like me and my family, I'm sure you can't imagine a New Year's Eve or a Sunday meal in the dead of winter without a side of black-eyed peas. What's nice about this stew is that it delivers a creamier and thicker base to this tried-and-true favorite, and it pairs well with my Sweet and Spicy Collard Greens (page 145).

1 (16-ounce) bag dried black-eyed peas, soaked in water to cover for 8 hours (overnight)
6 cups vegetable broth
3 cups ½-inch chunks peeled sweet potatoes
2 cups chopped yellow and/or red bell peppers
1½ cups finely diced onions
2 tablespoons minced garlic

1 cup medium salsa
1 tablespoon ground cumin
2 teaspoons smoked paprika
1 teaspoon salt, plus more as needed
1 teaspoon freshly ground black pepper
Cooked rice, for serving
Jalapeño Corn Bread (page 137) or your favorite corn bread, for serving

DRAIN the black-eyed peas and rinse them well. Place them in a large pot and add the vegetable broth. Bring to a rolling boil, reduce the heat to a low simmer, cover, and cook for 1 hour.

ADD the sweet potatoes, bell peppers, onions, garlic, salsa, cumin, smoked paprika, salt, and black pepper. Stir well and return to a boil. Once boiling, reduce the heat to medium-low, partially cover to let steam escape, and cook just until the sweet potatoes are tender, 15 to 20 minutes. Taste and add more salt if needed.

SERVE hot over rice, with Jalapeño Corn Bread on the side.

BRUSSELS RIGATONI CARBONARA

Serves 4 to 6

Gently charred Brussels sprouts add a hearty flavor to this carbonara, which is brimming with garlic, vegan butter, and a healthy dose of my vegan bacon for a full bacon-esque experience.

Sea salt
1 pound rigatoni pasta
8 tablespoons vegan butter
½ pound Brussels sprouts, trimmed and quartered
6 Slutty Strips, or vegan bacon of choice

½ teaspoon garlic powder
6 tablespoons vegan cream
5 garlic cloves, thinly sliced
1 cup grated vegan Parmesan cheese
½ cup diced pimentos
Shaved vegan Parmesan cheese (optional)

IN a large pot of boiling salted water, cook the rigatoni until al dente according to package directions. Drain the pasta in a colander.

IN a large skillet, melt 6 tablespoons of the butter over medium heat. Add the Brussels sprouts and cook, agitating the pan occasionally, until the edges of the leaves are slightly charred, about 8 to 10 minutes.

STIR in the bacon, garlic powder, and ½ teaspoon salt until the seasonings are well blended. Remove from the heat and set aside.

IN a large sauce pan, combine the cream, garlic, Parmesan, and remaining 2 tablespoons butter and bring to a simmer. Stir until the sauce thickens.

STIR in the cooked pasta and the Brussels sprouts/bacon mixture. Add the diced pimentos for color and shaved Parmesan, if desired, before you buss it down!

CAMPFIRE STEW

Serves 4 to 6

The perfect meal for a cold, wintry day, this stew is chock-full of vegan sausage links, beef-steak tomatoes, and warming spices. It will fill you up and warm your soul all at the same time.

½ cup vegetable oil
3 large vegan sausage links, halved horizontally
2 shallots, diced
1 celery stalk, diced
4 large beefsteak tomatoes, chopped
½ cup packed light brown sugar
1 teaspoon dried sage

1 teaspoon onion powder
Pinch of ground mace
1 (15-ounce) can black beans, drained and rinsed
¾ cup vegetable broth
Salt and freshly ground black pepper
1 tablespoon chopped green onion

PLACE a cast-iron skillet directly over an open flame (a campfire is preferable, but a stove will do).

WHEN the skillet is hot, add the vegetable oil. Then add the sausages and cook until the edges are seared, about 5 minutes. Remove and set aside.

ADD the shallots and celery and cook until they have slightly browned in color, about 5 minutes.

STIR in the tomatoes, brown sugar, sage, onion powder, and mace. Cook, stirring frequently, until the liquid from the tomatoes is reduced by half.

ADD the black beans and vegetable broth. Bring to a light simmer and return the sausage to the pan. Season with salt and pepper to taste.

TRANSFER to serving bowls, topping each with some of the green onion, and enjoy by the fire.

FRENCH-ISH ONION SOUP

Serves 6

This French-ish onion soup gives you all the joy of this cold weather favorite and still packs in the flavor with the simple substitutes of vegan butter, vegan broth, Marmite, and a dry white wine of your choice.

SOUP:
¼ cup plus 1 tablespoon extra-virgin olive oil
6 large yellow onions, thinly sliced (root to stem)
2 tablespoons vegan butter
¼ teaspoon salt
1 teaspoon sugar
2 garlic cloves, minced
3 tablespoons Marmite
½ cup dry vermouth or dry white wine
8 cups vegan broth
2 bay leaves

4 sprigs fresh thyme
½ teaspoon freshly ground black pepper
2 tablespoons brandy (optional)

CHEESE TOASTS:
3 slices rye or sourdough bread
Extra-virgin olive oil
1½ cups grated vegan Swiss cheese

FOR SERVING:
Grated vegan Parmesan cheese

MAKE THE SOUP: In a Dutch oven, heat the ¼ cup olive oil over medium-low heat. Add the onions and stir to coat with the oil. Cook until the onions are fork-tender, about 15 minutes.

ADD the remaining 1 tablespoon olive oil and the butter and mix until the onions are well coated. Cook over medium-high heat for 20 more minutes.

ADD the salt and sugar, stirring frequently to prevent sticking, until the onions reach a nice brown hue, about an additional 15 minutes.

STIR in the garlic and Marmite and cook, stirring, for 2 minutes, then immediately pour in the vermouth to deglaze the pan. Add the broth, bay leaves, thyme, and pepper, stirring gently. Cover the pot and cook for 30 minutes.

REMOVE the bay leaves and add the brandy, if desired. Add more salt and/or pepper to taste.

MAKE THE CHEESE TOASTS: Preheat the oven to 400°F.

Continued on next page

PLACE the bread on a sheet pan and brush generously with olive oil. Bake until the bread is lightly toasted, about 5 minutes. Flip each piece over and cover each generously with the cheese. Leave the oven on but set the broiler to high.

LADLE the soup and onions into six 2-cup broiler-proof bowls. Cut the cheese toasts in half and place a half on top of each bowl. Place the bowls on a baking sheet and set under the broiler until the cheese is melted, about 45 seconds. Remove from the oven. Be careful as the contents will be extremely hot.

PLACE each bowl on a small plate, add a sprinkle of Parmesan, and enjoy it while it's hot!

EGGPLANT PARM MARINARA FRIES

Serves 2

Eggplant Parm is always the way to go when you need some surefire comfort food—but it takes a lot of work to assemble. My recipe gives you the same cheese and marinara flavors but in the form of simple panko-coated eggplant fries.

Cooking spray
1 medium eggplant
6 tablespoons vegan egg substitute
1 cup grated vegan Parmesan cheese
½ cup panko bread crumbs
2 teaspoons garlic powder
2 teaspoons onion powder

2 teaspoons dried oregano
¾ teaspoon salt
½ teaspoon freshly ground black pepper
¾ cup homemade or store-bought marinara sauce, for dipping

POSITION a rack in the top third of the oven and preheat the oven to 420°F. Mist two baking sheets with generous amounts of cooking spray.

CUT the ends off the eggplant and peel it. Stand the eggplant up and slice it lengthwise into ½-inch-thick slabs. Then lay each slab down and cut it lengthwise into ½-inch-wide sticks. Then cut the sticks into 3-inch lengths.

SET up a dredging station: Place the egg substitute in a shallow bowl and whisk. In a second shallow bowl, combine the Parmesan, panko, garlic powder, onion powder, oregano, salt, and pepper. (Remove half of the Parm/panko mixture and set aside. Use it to refresh the panko bowl as needed; as you dredge the eggplant, the wet egg substitute can make the panko topping wet and clumpy.) Set the eggplant to the left of the two bowls and put the prepared baking sheets at the end of the line.

CAREFULLY place each eggplant strip in the egg substitute. Then submerge it in the panko bowl, pressing to make sure it adheres on all sides. Finally place the fries on the prepared baking sheet, leaving space between them.

BAKE until browned and crispy, 15 to 20 minutes.

USE a wide spatula to remove the eggplant from the baking sheet, scraping the bottom of the pan while lifting them up to ensure the coating stays intact.

SERVE with the marinara sauce for dunking.

FRIED GREEN TOMATOES

Serves 2 to 4

Fried green tomatoes take a little work before you get 'em to the plate, but learning how to master this classic Southern appetizer will be well worth the effort when you add these to your small-bites menu.

BREADING MIX:
1 cup all-purpose flour
1 tablespoon freshly cracked black pepper
1 teaspoon sweet paprika
1 teaspoon onion powder
1 teaspoon garlic powder
½ teaspoon ground ginger
1 teaspoon salt

BATTER:
1 cup vegan cream
1 tablespoon freshly cracked black pepper
1 teaspoon sweet paprika
1 teaspoon onion powder
1 teaspoon garlic powder
½ teaspoon ground ginger
Juice of ½ lemon

BREAD CRUMB TOPPING:
1 cup vegan bread crumbs
½ teaspoon freshly cracked black pepper
½ teaspoon sweet paprika
½ teaspoon onion powder
½ teaspoon garlic powder
¼ teaspoon red pepper flakes

Sunflower oil, for frying
2 green tomatoes, cut into slices ¼ inch thick

DIPPING SAUCE:
½ cup vegan mayonnaise
1 teaspoon smoked paprika
2 tablespoons fresh lemon juice

MAKE THE BREADING MIX: In a shallow bowl, combine the flour, pepper, paprika, onion powder, garlic powder, ginger, and salt. Set aside.

MAKE THE BATTER: In a shallow bowl, combine the cream, pepper, paprika, onion powder, garlic powder, ginger, and lemon juice. Set aside.

MAKE THE BREAD CRUMB TOPPING. In another shallow bowl, combine the bread crumbs, pepper, paprika, onion powder, garlic powder, and red pepper flakes. Set aside.

INTO a deep saucepan, pour 2 inches of oil and heat over medium heat until shimmering.

SET up a dredging station in this order: Plate of tomatoes, bowl of breading, bowl of batter, bowl of bread crumbs. Dredge the tomato slices first in the breading, then the batter, and finally the bread crumb mixture. Shake off any excess during each step.

WORKING in batches of two at a time, gently place the battered green tomatoes in the hot oil. Fry until golden brown, about 5 minutes. Drain on a rack or paper towel.

MAKE THE DIPPING SAUCE: In a small bowl, combine the mayonnaise, smoked paprika, and lemon juice.

PLATE the tomatoes, add the sauce on the side, and enjoy while they're warm!

GNOCCHI FLORENTINE

Serves 6

Homestyle gnocchi Florentine is a comfort classic packed with potatoes, mushrooms, garlic, and spinach. Learning how to form your gnocchi into nice-size portions will take some practice, but once you master this recipe, it will definitely be your go-to meal on a cool autumn evening.

GNOCCHI:

3 pounds white or Russet potatoes, unpeeled

3½ cups all-purpose flour

1 teaspoon salt, plus more as needed

¼ teaspoon freshly ground black pepper

FLORENTINE SAUCE:

1 teaspoon extra-virgin olive oil

3 garlic cloves, chopped

3 tablespoons cornstarch

1 cup vegan cream, chilled

½ cup vegetable broth

10 ounces cremini (baby bella) mushrooms, sliced

2 tablespoons nutritional yeast

1 teaspoon fresh lime juice

6 ounces fresh spinach

Salt

MAKE THE GNOCCHI: In a large saucepan of boiling water, cook the potatoes until fork-tender, about 20 minutes. Drain and when cool enough to handle, peel them, place in a large bowl, and mash until smooth.

ADD the flour to the potatoes, mixing in a little at a time until the dough is no longer sticky.

ADD the salt and pepper and continue kneading until you have a smooth ball of dough with no lumps or clumps.

BRING a large pot of salted water to a boil.

FORM balls the size of the tip of your thumb and gently roll a fork over each ball, creating an imprint of 4 lines.

START THE FLORENTINE SAUCE: In a large skillet, heat the olive oil and garlic over medium heat.

GENTLY drop the gnocchi into the boiling water and cook until they rise to the top. Scoop them out of the water with a slotted spoon and toss them immediately into the skillet of warmed oil.

Continued on next page

SAUTÉ the gnocchi until golden brown, about 10 minutes.

MEANWHILE, in a small bowl, vigorously whisk the cornstarch into the chilled cream.

ADD the broth to the pan of gnocchi, then immediately add the cream/cornstarch mixture and bring to a simmer.

ADD the nutritional yeast, lime juice, mushrooms, and spinach. Reduce the heat to medium and simmer until the mushrooms are soft and lightly browned and the spinach is wilted and bright green, 3 to 5 minutes. Season with salt to taste.

SERVE and enjoy!

MAPLE-ROASTED VEGETABLES

Serves 4

Your favorite root vegetables will take a sweet turn in this roasted vegetable medley that includes sweet onions, parsnips, beets, sweet potatoes, and Yukon Golds coated in pure maple syrup.

2 Yukon Gold potatoes, cut into 1½-inch pieces

1 large sweet potato, peeled and cut into 1½-inch pieces

2 parsnips, peeled and cut into 2-inch lengths

3 beets, peeled and cut into 1½-inch pieces

2 large sweet onions, peeled and quartered

½ cup grapeseed oil

½ cup pure maple syrup

2 garlic cloves, minced

Salt and freshly ground black pepper

PREHEAT the oven to 350°F.

ARRANGE the vegetables in a single layer on one or two large sheet pans.

IN a small bowl, stir together the oil, maple syrup, and garlic and pour over the vegetables. Toss to combine the oil mixture with the veggies and then spread them once again in a single layer on the pan(s). Season with salt and pepper to taste.

BAKE until the vegetables are tender and a little caramelized from the syrup, about 1 hour.

TRANSFER to a bowl and serve immediately.

JALAPEÑO CORN BREAD

Makes 9 pieces

Your corn bread is going to a whole other level with this recipe, which includes flaxseed, almond milk, and just enough jalapeños to get your taste buds jumping.

Vegetable oil, for the pan
2 tablespoons ground flaxseed
¼ cup plus 1 tablespoon water
1 cup all-purpose flour
1 cup cornmeal
1 tablespoon plus 1 teaspoon baking powder
½ cup sugar
1 teaspoon salt
¼ cup grapeseed oil
1 cup unsweetened almond milk
¼ cup corn kernels
2 medium jalapeños, sliced and seeded
¼ cup shredded vegan cheddar cheese

PREHEAT the oven to 425°F. Lightly oil an 8-inch square baking pan.

IN a small bowl, whisk together the ground flaxseed and water. Set aside for 5 minutes.

IN a large bowl, thoroughly combine the flour, cornmeal, baking powder, sugar, and salt.

ADD the grapeseed oil, milk, flaxseed mixture, jalapeños, and corn kernels to the flour mixture and mix by hand until combined. Pour the batter into the prepared pan and top with the jalapeños.

BAKE until the edges of the corn bread turn golden brown and a toothpick inserted into the center comes out clean, 18 to 20 minutes.

REMOVE from the oven and sprinkle the cheese over the still-warm corn bread. Allow to cool before cutting into nine equal squares and serving.

MUSTARD-SAUTÉED GREEN BEANS

Serves 2

These ain't your mama's green beans! My sautéed green beans get a fresh hot remix with mustard seeds, cumin, and a bit of Sriracha. For a pop of color, garnish with a sprinkle of mixed microgreens.

Kosher salt
2 cups green beans
4 teaspoons peanut oil
6 shallots, thinly sliced
2 teaspoons mustard seeds
1 teaspoon ground coriander

¼ teaspoon ground cumin
Sea salt and freshly ground black pepper
½ cup vegetable broth
1 teaspoon vegan white wine
¼ teaspoon Sriracha sauce

SET up a large bowl of ice and water and add 1 tablespoon kosher salt.

IN a medium pot, bring 4 cups water to a boil and add 1 tablespoon kosher salt.

ADD the beans to the boiling water and cook until they are crisp-tender, about 2 minutes. Drain and immediately submerge them in the ice bath until cool to the touch, about 45 seconds. Drain them again and set aside.

MEANWHILE, in a large nonstick skillet, heat the oil over medium heat. Add the shallots and mustard seeds and cook, stirring occasionally, until the shallots are softened and golden, about 12 minutes. Stir in the coriander, cumin, and a pinch each of sea salt and pepper and cook for 45 seconds. Stir in the green beans and vegetable broth and cook until the broth evaporates.

STIR in the wine and Sriracha and serve immediately.

OKRA SALAD

Serves 4

My version of okra salad delivers a mouthwatering kick to this Southern staple. By cooking the okra lightly and combining it with fresh cabbage, tomato, carrots, and bell pepper, you will have a new appreciation for this vegetable and keep this salad in your regular party rotation.

¾ cup rice vinegar
¼ cup packed light brown sugar
2 pounds fresh okra, washed and
  halved lengthwise
1 cup shredded red cabbage
1 medium tomato, cut into wedges

½ cup shredded carrots
½ yellow bell pepper, sliced
1 teaspoon red pepper flakes
Pinch of freshly ground black pepper

IN a large bowl, whisk together the vinegar and brown sugar until well incorporated.

ADD the okra, cabbage, tomato, carrots, bell pepper, red pepper flakes, and black pepper and toss to fully coat the vegetables.

ENJOY immediately or refrigerate for a few hours to enjoy the married flavors.

POTATO MUSHROOM SOUP

Serves 4

You won't get stuck in a slump of the same winter soups with this winner. This soup combines cremini mushrooms and red potatoes into a delectable blend that will fill you up and keep you warm on even the coldest winter night.

2 tablespoons sunflower oil
1 large yellow onion, diced
2 medium celery stalks, chopped
2 medium carrots, sliced
5 garlic cloves, chopped
2 tablespoons tomato paste
¼ cup all-purpose flour
1 to 2 teaspoon Marmite, to taste
1 cup dry red vegan wine
2 pounds red potatoes, unpeeled, cut into 1- to 2-inch chunks

4 cups vegetable broth
2 teaspoons fresh thyme leaves
2 tablespoons finely chopped fresh rosemary, plus 4 whole sprigs for garnish
1 pound cremini (baby bella) mushrooms, roughly chopped
Salt and freshly ground black pepper

IN a soup pot, heat the sunflower oil over medium heat. Add the onion, celery and carrots and cook, stirring occasionally, until the onion and celery are translucent and the carrot is fork-tender, about 15 minutes.

ADD the garlic and cook for 2 to 3 minutes.

ADD the tomato paste and stir to prevent sticking. Once all the vegetables are coated, sprinkle in the flour and cook for about 45 seconds, until the flour is fully incorporated. Immediately add the Marmite and wine, scraping the bottom to remove any stuck-on bits.

POUR in the potatoes and vegetable broth. Increase the heat to medium-high, cover, and bring to a boil. Reduce the heat to a simmer, then stir in the thyme, rosemary, and mushrooms. Let simmer until the potatoes are tender, about 20 minutes.

THE soup can be enjoyed chunky or blended with an immersion blender until smooth. Totally your call, just make sure you share it! Before serving, season with salt and pepper to taste, divide among four bowls, and garnish each with a rosemary sprig.

SWEET AND SPICY COLLARD GREENS

Serves 4 to 6

Sunni Speaks is a company that is striving to build the bridge between health and the hood by providing vegan versions of soul food classics. Their trademarked Smackin' Mac, which is a soy-free vegan baked mac and cheese, is their best-seller. In 2020, the company expanded to nationwide cold shipping to provide vegan soul food to every neighborhood, not just Atlanta, where the company was founded. The company has also become a vendor to some of Atlanta's most notable restaurants. In the future, Sunni Speaks plans to be the preferred vegan option in restaurants and grocery stores globally, but for now, Suneeta's biggest accomplishment is having her mom specifically request her collard greens at Thanksgiving.

4 cups water
¼ teaspoon liquid smoke
1 tablespoon vegetable bouillon base
1 yellow onion, sliced
4 garlic cloves, sliced
2 tablespoons onion powder
2 tablespoons garlic powder
1 tablespoon salt

1 teaspoon cayenne pepper, plus
  more for garnish
4 tablespoons vegan butter
2 (16-ounce) bags cut collard greens
¼ cup apple cider vinegar
¼ cup agave syrup
Freshly ground black pepper

IN a large pot, combine the water, liquid smoke, bouillon base, onion, sliced garlic, onion powder, garlic powder, salt, cayenne pepper, and butter. Bring to a simmer and cook until the onion and garlic soften, about 15 minutes.

ADD the collards, cover, and cook for 30 to 40 minutes.

STIR in the vinegar and agave syrup. Continue cooking to your desired tenderness for the collards.

TRANSFER to a serving bowl and garnish with freshly ground black pepper and a sprinkle of cayenne pepper. Serve immediately.

SPINACH AND MUSHROOM ALFREDO

Serves 4 to 6

A good Alfredo is most likely on your Cheat Day menu, but you can dive into this vegan version guilt free — with fewer calories and an easy vegan cheese substitute.

8 ounces dried fettuccine
1 medium white onion, diced
2 cups vegetable broth
8 garlic cloves, minced
2 tablespoons extra-virgin olive oil
2 cups spinach leaves
1 pound cremini mushrooms, sliced

8 ounces dried fettuccine
¾ cup roasted cashews
¼ cup nutritional yeast
1 tablespoon fresh lemon juice
1 teaspoon salt
½ teaspoon freshly ground black
   pepper

BRING a medium pot of salted water to a boil.

MEANWHILE, in a large skillet, cook the onion and 1 cup of the broth over medium-high heat until the onion is tender, about 8 minutes. Add the garlic and cook a couple of minutes more, stirring often.

IN another large skillet, heat the oil over medium heat until the oil shimmers. Add the spinach and mushrooms and cook until the spinach is wilted and bright green and the mushrooms are soft and lightly browned, 3 to 5 minutes.

ADD the fettuccine to the boiling water and cook according to the package directions. Drain.

SCRAPE the cooked onion/garlic mixture into a blender. Add ½ cup of the broth, the cashews, nutritional yeast, lemon juice, salt, and pepper and blend on high until very creamy and smooth. Add the remaining ½ cup of the broth, a little at a time, if needed to reach a consistency that can coat the pasta. Pour into the pan with the spinach and mushrooms and stir.

SERVE over the cooked fettuccine.

STUFFED BUTTERNUT SQUASH

Serves 4

Stuffed butternut squash is a great way to mix up your autumn vegetable game and works as a full meal because it's brimming with a filling made with brown rice, dried cranberries, walnuts, and mushrooms.

2 cups water
1 cup brown rice
3 tablespoons extra-virgin olive oil, plus more for drizzling
2 sprigs fresh rosemary
1 cup dried cranberries
1 (3-pound) butternut squash
1½ teaspoons sea salt
1 yellow onion, chopped

2 celery stalks, chopped
3 ounces mushrooms, sliced
½ cup walnuts, chopped
2 cups baby spinach
1 tablespoon fresh sage leaves, chopped
1 teaspoon garlic powder
1 teaspoon onion powder

IN a small saucepan, bring the water to a boil. Add the brown rice, 1 tablespoon of the olive oil, the rosemary, and dried cranberries. Cover, reduce the heat to medium-low, and simmer until the rice has absorbed all the liquid, about 35 minutes. Discard the rosemary stems.

MEANWHILE, preheat the oven to 375°F. Line a sheet pan with foil.

CUT the butternut squash in half lengthwise and scoop out the seeds. Drizzle the squash with 1 tablespoon of the olive oil and season with 1 teaspoon of the sea salt.

PLACE the squash cut side down on the prepared sheet pan and roast for 25 minutes.

FLIP the squash over and roast until almost fork-tender, about an additional 20 minutes. Remove the squash and set aside to cool, but leave the oven on.

ONCE the squash is cool to the touch, scoop out the flesh from the neck of the squash leaving a 1-inch border. Set the cooked squash flesh aside.

IN a large skillet, heat the remaining 1 tablespoon oil until hot. Add the onion, celery, mushrooms, and walnuts and cook until tender, about 5 minutes. Remove from the heat.

Continued on next page

ADD the spinach to the pan and gently stir until the spinach begins to slightly wilt from the residual heat in the pan. Stir in the rice mixture and the reserved squash flesh. Season with the sage, garlic powder, onion powder, and the remaining ½ teaspoon salt.

STUFF the rice mixture into the squash halves. Carefully flip one squash half on top of the other. Return the squash to the sheet pan and drizzle with olive oil. Bake until the squash is warm and tender throughout, an additional 15 minutes.

CAREFULLY pull apart the squash halves and transfer them to a serving platter. Gently fluff the rice mixture, mounding any that falls out on top of the halves.

SERVE the squash halves whole (so your guests can see all that beauty!), and cut them into slices at the table.

ZUCCHINI CAKES

Serves 2

These zucchini cakes are a fun play cousin to my Fried Green Tomatoes (page 130). The cakes take on a bold vegan twist with ripe bananas and dried cranberries for a bit of sweetness and tartness.

2 cups spelt flour
2 tablespoons date sugar
½ cup mashed ripe bananas
2 cups unsweetened almond milk
1 cup finely chopped zucchini
¼ cup dried cranberries, plus more for garnish (optional)

1 tablespoon sunflower oil, plus more as needed

FOR SERVING:
Sliced banana (optional)
Zucchini strips (optional)
Agave syrup or pure maple syrup

IN a bowl, combine the spelt flour and sugar. Add the mashed bananas and almond milk and stir until well combined. Stir in the zucchini and cranberries.

IN a large skillet, heat the oil over medium heat. Ladle small amounts of the zucchini batter into the pan. Cook for 1 minute, flip, and repeat. Continue until all the batter is used, adding more oil to the pan as needed.

SERVE immediately, garnished with dried cranberries, sliced banana, and zucchini strips, if desired. Serve the agave syrup on the side.

FIVE

DA BUTTERS, DA DIPS, DA JAMS, AND DA JELLIES

Just because you go vegan doesn't mean that you don't like to SOP up your plate like you would with any good dip, jam, jelly, or gravy. Many of the staple dishes within this cookbook will be enhanced and enjoyed even more with just a dollop of some of these great dips and garnishes, which take them over the top.

While I was growing up in Maryland, there was nothing better than going to our crab feast and dipping a juicy crab leg into some butter or tartar sauce for an extra kick. The recipes in this chapter definitely come with a lot of kick, spice, and punch to give your new vegan favorites a whole lot of soul. Some of my favorites include Apricot Jam (page 158), which goes well on everything from Sunday morning biscuits to a nice garnish for your charcuterie board. I also love the Peanut Satay Dipping Sauce (page 164), which is great for shrimp or vegan kebabs. And my Spinach Artichoke Dip (page 170) will have you enjoying this party classic without sacrificing any of the taste.

APPLE BUTTER

Makes 9 cups

Are you really doing your autumn favorites right without some apple butter? If you aren't already down with the goodness that is my apple butter, do you yourself a favor: Get up into this recipe and put it on everything from fresh-baked breads to your favorite fruits and desserts.

4 pounds apples, unpeeled, cored and diced
2 cups apple juice
2 cups evaporated cane juice, or to taste

1 ½ teaspoons ground cinnamon
¼ teaspoon ground allspice
2 teaspoons fresh lemon juice

IN a large pot, combine the apples and apple juice. Cover and cook over low heat until soft, about 20 minutes. Puree with an immersion blender or in batches in a food processor until smooth.

ADD enough evaporated cane juice to sweeten to your taste. Add the cinnamon, allspice, and lemon juice. Stir well. Uncover and continue cooking over low heat until the mixture thickens to a spreadable consistency.

TRANSFER the apple butter to a stainless steel bowl, set aside, and let it come to room temperature.

MEANWHILE, sterilize four 16-ounce mason jars by boiling them in water for 10 minutes. Dry thoroughly.

POUR the apple butter into the still-hot sterilized jars. You'll have about a cup left over, which you can eat right away or store in another airtight container.

REFRIGERATE for 1 hour before placing the lids on top. Then refrigerate for up to 1 week, or freeze for up to 1 year.

ENJOY over toast or straight from the jar!

APRICOT JAM

Makes 10 cups

I like to think of apricot jam as apple butter's lighter and flirtier cousin. While the jam takes a little more love and care on the stovetop, once it's done it's the perfect topping for your biscuits and pancakes.

3 pounds fresh apricots, pitted and
  chopped
2¼ cups sugar

½ teaspoon ground cinnamon
½ teaspoon ground mace
Pinch of ground ginger

IN a large saucepan, combine the apricots, sugar, cinnamon, mace, and ginger. Set over medium-low heat. The juices should slowly extract from the fruit and begin to simmer. Stirring frequently, increase the heat to medium-high and cook for 45 minutes. As the fruit breaks down, continue to stir the mixture to prevent it from sticking to the bottom.

TRANSFER the jam to a stainless steel bowl, set aside, and let it come to room temperature.

MEANWHILE, sterilize ten 8-ounce mason jars by boiling them in water for 10 minutes. Dry thoroughly.

POUR the jam into the still-hot sterilized jars.

REFRIGERATE for 1 hour before placing the lids on top. Then refrigerate for up to 1 week, or freeze for up to 1 year.

ENJOY your jam on biscuits or pancakes!

CRANBERRY RELISH

Makes 3 cups

When you need a nice dose of tart and sweet for your morning oatmeal or a sweet kick for a savory soup, this cranberry relish is the sho nuff winner. The green apple adds to the tartness, and the pecans finish off this simple topping with a warm nuttiness.

2 cups fresh cranberries
1 small green apple
1 medium orange

½ cup pecans
½ cup evaporated cane juice, or to
    taste

RINSE and sort the cranberries to remove the mushy ones.

CUT the apple into quarters and remove the core.

PEEL half the orange, leaving half the peel on. Cut the orange into chunks.

IN a food processor, combine the cranberries, apple, orange, and pecans and pulse lightly. The mixture should be finely chopped, but not pureed. Transfer to a large bowl and fold in the evaporated cane juice to sweeten to your taste. The relish should be tart, but not sour or bitter.

COVER with plastic wrap and refrigerate for at least 1 hour before using. The cranberry relish can be refrigerated in an airtight container for up to 1 week.

FONDUE CHEESE BOWL

Serves 4

You don't have to miss out on this cheesy favorite EVER again! Simply add whatever vegan cheese you feel like and punch it up with a vegan beer, and you are back in business with a fondue that will definitely be a crowd-pleaser.

1 large round loaf vegan bread
4 tablespoons vegan butter, melted
1 cup shredded vegan cheese
1 cup water

1 cup vegan beer
Salt
Parsley, for garnish

PREHEAT the oven to 375°F.

MAKE the lid in the bread by cutting in a circular direction all the way around (like cutting off the top of a pumpkin). Tear out the interior in small chunks, place in a serving bowl, and set aside.

BRUSH the bread lid and inside of the bowl with the melted butter. Set the bread bowl on a baking sheet and bake for 7 minutes, or until the bread looks toasted.

MEANWHILE, in a small saucepan, stir together the cheese and water and bring to a light simmer. Once the cheese is thoroughly incorporated, add the beer, ¼ cup at a time, until the thickness is as desired. Add salt to taste. Reduce the heat.

REMOVE the bread bowl from the oven. Pour the cheese mixture into the bowl, garnish with parsley, serve immediately with the bread chunks, and dip away!

HOMEMADE VEGAN GARLIC BUTTER

Makes 2 cups

My vegan garlic butter is the best way to add a boost to your favorite dishes. Enjoy this spread cold or warm; it pairs well with everything from my Roasted Purple Sweet Potatoes (page 51) to my "Bacon"-Wrapped Asparagus (page 79).

1 cup refined coconut oil, melted
½ cup canned butter beans, drained and rinsed
½ cup unsweetened nondairy yogurt
⅓ cup extra-virgin olive oil

2 garlic cloves, chopped
2½ teaspoons nutritional yeast
1 teaspoon apple cider vinegar
1 teaspoon sugar
½ teaspoon salt

IN a blender, combine the coconut oil, beans, yogurt, olive oil, garlic, nutritional yeast, vinegar, sugar, and salt and blend until smooth. Pour into a glass container and refrigerate until it is firm.

THE garlic butter can be stored in an airtight glass container in the refrigerator for up to 1 week. When you're ready to use it, remove it from the refrigerator to come to room temperature so that it will be spreadable.

PEANUT SATAY DIPPING SAUCE

Makes 3 cups

This sauce right here?! My peanut satay dipping sauce is EVERYTHING, and it's a great complement to roasted veggies and fried or baked tofu.

½ cup packed light brown sugar
¼ cup rice vinegar
2 cups creamy peanut butter
½ cup grapeseed oil

½ cup coconut milk
1 tablespoon red pepper flakes
  (optional)

IN a bowl, stir together the brown sugar and vinegar until the sugar is partially dissolved.

ADD the peanut butter and whisk until well incorporated. Drizzle in the grapeseed oil and continue to whisk until the mixture becomes thick and shiny.

SLOWLY add some of the coconut milk a bit at time until you have reached your desired consistency for a dipping sauce. If you want to turn this delicious dip into a salad dressing, add more coconut milk.

IF desired, spice things up a notch with the pepper flakes.

THE dipping sauce can be stored in an airtight container and refrigerated for up to 1 week.

PIMENTO CHEESE SPREAD

Makes 2 cups

Pimento peppers are an acquired taste that your mouth may take a minute to warm up to. But after you combine them into this easy cheese spread, you will be spreading it on everything from crusty vegan breads, to olives and peppers, to your favorite veggie sandwiches.

12 ounces vegan cream cheese
4 ounces vegan mayonnaise
1 cup vegan shredded sharp cheddar cheese
2 ounces chopped pimento peppers, drained
1 ounce dried chives
1 tablespoon onion powder
1 teaspoon garlic powder
1 teaspoon sweet paprika

IN a bowl, combine the cream cheese and mayo until well incorporated.

ADD the cheddar, pimentos, chives, onion powder, garlic powder, and paprika. Mix until well incorporated. The mixture should be chunky and thin, but thick enough to stand up on a cracker.

THE pimento cheese spread can be stored in an airtight container in the fridge for up to 1 week.

PINEAPPLE SALSA

Makes 2 cups

One spoonful of this irresistible pineapple salsa will take all of your grilled summer favorites from just aight to WOW! It is especially good with the BBQ Tofu Bowl (page 74), Backyard Quesadillas (page 80), and Fajita Tacos (page 33).

1 ripe pineapple, cored and cut into large cubes
½ cup packed dark brown sugar
½ cup rice vinegar
2 tomatoes, seeded and diced

3 garlic cloves, diced
1 bunch green onions, thinly sliced
1 bunch basil, leaves hand torn, plus a few whole leaves for garnish

IN a large bowl, combine the pineapple and brown sugar. Mix until the pineapple is coated with the sugar, then add the vinegar. Add the tomatoes, garlic, and green onions and mix thoroughly.

SET aside for up to 2 hours to let the flavors marinate.

WHEN ready to serve, transfer the salsa to a serving bowl and add the torn basil leaves. Mix to incorporate. Garnish with a few whole basil leaves.

SPINACH ARTICHOKE DIP

Serves 4 to 6

Your small bites won't be right without a good spinach artichoke dip. This all-vegan take on the party classic will give you all the bite and spice without sacrificing texture or flavor, and it's a great match for your favorite vegan chips or crackers.

10 ounces vegan cream cheese
½ cup vegan mayonnaise
½ cup vegan sour cream
1 (10-ounce) package frozen chopped spinach, defrosted and drained
6 ounces marinated artichokes, chopped
2 cups shredded vegan Monterey Jack cheese

1 cup packed shredded vegan mozzarella cheese
½ cup dried onions
1 tablespoon garlic powder
½ teaspoon kosher salt
½ teaspoon freshly cracked pepper
½ teaspoon red pepper flakes

IN a large bowl, combine the cream cheese, mayo, and sour cream.

ADD the spinach, artichokes, both cheeses, the onions, garlic powder, kosher salt, black pepper, and red pepper flakes and gently fold together.

THE dip should be thick enough to form stiff peaks when you lift your spatula from the bowl.

TRANSFER to a bowl and serve.

ENJOY!

I couldn't let you create a whole vegan feast without giving you some bomb treats to finish out your meal. I know that as you transition into a vegan lifestyle, thoughtfully including desserts and/or foods with a lot of sugar can be of concern, especially for those who—like a lot of my customers—are diabetic or prediabetic. The recipes in this chapter have been curated to help you satisfy your sweeter side while still keeping your health and fitness goals in check. If you want to go lighter, I would start with the Grilled Plums (page 178) and the Watermelon Creamsicles (page 186).

If you have a little more room in your stomach or a bit more of a sweet tooth, you can't go wrong with the Sweet Bun Desert (page 184), which is one of my favorite Jamaican desserts from my family's recipe book, or the Sweet Potato Pudding (page 185), which is a nice twist on the traditional sweet potato pie.

And remember, you don't have to make dessert feel torturous or beat yourself up about having a slice of cake or pie. It's all about balance, and this chapter is here to round out my other beautiful recipes with some sweet treats that will shore be pleasing to both you and those you love.

RAW VEGAN CHOCOLATE MOUSSE

Serves 4

I know I'm biased, but this dessert is kinda fire, if I do say so myself. The dark cocoa powder gives the mousse a rich, deep foundation, and then ground ginger, agave syrup, mandarin orange, and cinnamon continue to excite the palate. What other chocolate mousse is giving you this much flavor?

2 large avocados, halved and pitted
1½ cups dark cocoa powder
1 cup vegan cream
½ cup cold-brewed raspberry-flavored tea
1 tablespoon agave syrup
1 mandarin orange, peeled and segmented (pith removed)
½ teaspoon ground cinnamon
½ teaspoon ground ginger

10 ounces gingerbread cookies, crumbled
Vegan dark chocolate chips, for garnish

ADDITIONAL GARNISHES, OPTIONAL:
⅓ cup fresh blueberries
⅓ cup fresh pomegranate seeds
4 ounces coconut whipped cream

SCOOP the avocado flesh into a food processor. Add the cocoa powder, cream, tea, agave syrup, orange, cinnamon, and ginger and blend until smooth. Scrape down the sides and blend again.

TRANSFER to an airtight container and cover with plastic wrap. The wrap should touch the top of the mousse so a film does not form. Chill for at least 2 hours before serving.

TO serve, divide the cookie crumbles among four glasses or serving bowls and top each with some chocolate chips and, if desired, blueberries, pomegranate seeds, and whipped cream.

GRILLED PLUMS

Serves 3 or 4

Don't sleep on these grilled plums! They are a super-simple and healthy addition to a summer night hang and a guilt-free way to please your sweet tooth.

2 tablespoons vegan butter, melted
6 plums, halved and pitted
¼ cup vegan caramel
4 cups coconut whipped cream

½ teaspoon kosher salt
2 sprigs fresh mint, leaves cut into a chiffonade

HEAT your grill to medium-high.

BRUSH the melted butter over the plums and grill cut side down for 1 minute or until grill marks appear.

IN a bowl, gently fold the caramel into the whipped cream until it is lightly swirled in.

SPOON the whipped cream mixture on top of the plums, grilled side up, and sprinkle with the kosher salt and mint. Enjoy immediately.

FUDGY BROWNIES

Makes 9 brownies

Who doesn't love a good brownie? And this one is ready for whipped cream or ice cream — or both!

Softened vegan butter for the pan
1 ½ cups cane sugar
8 tablespoons vegan butter, melted
⅓ cup unsweetened almond milk
1 tablespoon pure vanilla extract

1 cup all-purpose flour
¾ cup unsweetened cocoa powder
1 teaspoon baking powder
½ teaspoon salt
1 cup vegan chocolate chips

PREHEAT the oven to 350°F. Line an 8-inch square baking pan with parchment paper so that there is an overhang on two sides of the pan. Grease the parchment paper with some softened butter.

IN a large bowl, whisk together the sugar and melted butter. Whisk in the milk and vanilla.

IN a medium bowl, combine the flour, cocoa powder, baking powder, and salt.

MIX the flour mixture into the butter/sugar mixture until well combined. Fold in the chocolate chips.

SPREAD the batter evenly into the prepared baking pan.

BAKE until a fork inserted into the center comes out clean, 25 to 30 minutes.

LET cool for 30 minutes in the pan. Then grab the parchment paper handles and pull the brownies out. Set on a wire rack and allow to cool completely before cutting into 9 equal squares.

ENJOY!

DEE'S FAMOUS PEANUT BUTTER COOKIES

Makes 24 cookies

These cookies combine two great loves—cookies and peanut butter! They have a great texture and are just waiting for your favorite nondairy milk.

3 cups all-purpose flour
1 teaspoon baking soda
1 teaspoon baking powder
½ teaspoon salt
1 cup creamy peanut butter

16 tablespoons (2 sticks) vegan butter
1 cup granulated cane sugar
1 cup packed light brown sugar
1 teaspoon pure vanilla extract
6 tablespoons canned chickpea liquid

PREHEAT the oven to 350°F. Line a baking sheet with parchment paper.

IN a medium bowl, combine the flour, baking soda, baking powder, and salt and set aside.

USING a stand mixer, cream together the peanut butter, butter, granulated cane sugar, brown sugar, and vanilla until light and fluffy. Beat in the chickpea liquid 3 tablespoons at a time until well combined. Stir in the flour mixture until fully incorporated. Do not overmix.

USING a cookie scoop, place dough ½ inch apart on the prepared baking sheet. Bake the cookies until the edges are brown, 12 to 14 minutes, then transfer to a wire rack to cool.

ENJOY!

SOUTHERN PEACH COBBLER

Serves 8

Yes, even you can make a holiday-worthy peach cobbler. And there will be no canned peaches here! Your biscuits will be buttery and flaky, and everything will come together perfectly. Beware: This may become your signature holiday dish!

PEACH FILLING:
8 cups sliced peeled peaches (8 to 9 peaches)
½ cup packed light brown sugar
2 tablespoons cornstarch
1 tablespoon fresh lemon juice
1 teaspoon ground cinnamon
½ teaspoon salt

BISCUIT:
1½ cups all-purpose flour
½ cup granulated sugar, plus more for sprinkling
1 teaspoon baking powder
½ teaspoon baking soda
½ teaspoon salt
8 tablespoons vegan butter, cut into cubes
¼ cup unsweetened almond milk, plus more as needed
Ground cinnamon, for sprinkling
Strawberries and raspberries or fruit of choice, for garnish

PREHEAT the oven to 375°F.

MAKE THE PEACH FILLING: Place the peaches in a 7 × 11-inch baking dish. Add the brown sugar, cornstarch, lemon juice, cinnamon, and salt and toss gently until well coated.

BAKE for about 10 minutes. Remove from the oven and set aside to cool. Leave the oven on.

MAKE THE BISCUIT: In a bowl, combine the flour, granulated sugar, baking powder, baking soda, and salt. Using your fingers, cut the butter into the flour mixture until it resembles coarse crumbs. Add the almond milk and stir together until a stiff dough has formed. You may need to add a little more milk. If so, add it 1 to 2 teaspoons at a time.

DROP pieces of dough onto the peach filling so that it is mostly covered. Brush a little milk over the biscuits and sprinkle with a little sugar and a dusting of cinnamon.

BAKE until the filling is bubbling and the biscuits are golden brown, 45 minutes to 1 hour. Remove from the oven and let sit for at least 20 minutes.

SERVE garnished with strawberries and raspberries or fruit of choice.

SWEET BUN DESSERT

Serves 4

This is a dessert that you should definitely share with your peeps who have a sense of adventure and aren't afraid to shake up their sweet tooths. Filled with cinnamon, nutmeg, coconut whipped cream, fresh berries, and cayenne pepper, your guests will still be gushing about how much they love it well after their bellies are filled with this delight.

Peanut oil, for frying
2 tablespoons plus 1 teaspoon sugar
1 teaspoon ground cinnamon
1 teaspoon ground nutmeg
1 teaspoon cayenne pepper

1 cup coconut whipped cream
4 vegan bao buns
2 strawberries, sliced
3 small sprigs fresh mint, for garnish
½ cup blueberries, for garnish

IN a deep saucepan, heat 1 inch of oil to 375°F.

MEANWHILE, in a small bowl, mix together the sugar and ½ teaspoon each of the cinnamon, nutmeg, and cayenne pepper.

IN a medium bowl, gently fold the remaining ½ teaspoon each cinnamon, nutmeg, and cayenne pepper into the coconut whipped cream.

LOWER the buns into the hot oil and cook for 5 seconds on each side or until lightly browned. Remove the buns from the oven and immediately toss in the sugar-spice mixture to coat.

WHILE still warm, spoon the spiced whipped cream inside the buns. Serve garnished with the mint sprigs and blueberries. Enjoy immediately.

SWEET POTATO PUDDING

Serves 4

Sweet potato pudding is a great alternative to bread pudding and a lighter take on the classic Southern pie. With just six ingredients, this will easily become one of your new fall favorites.

½ cup rolled oats

½ cup nondairy milk

1 cup peeled, cubed sweet potatoes, boiled until fork-tender

1 tablespoon pure maple syrup

1 tablespoon ginger syrup

¼ teaspoon pure vanilla extract

IN a blender, combine the oats, milk, sweet potatoes, maple syrup, ginger syrup, and vanilla and pulse until smooth.

POUR the pudding into four individual cups. Chill for at least 2 hours before serving.

WATERMELON CREAMSICLES

Makes 4 pops

Nothing brings back the childhood joy of a good summer hang like a creamsicle! These watermelon creamsicles combine the brightness of fresh lemon and mint, the smoothness of coconut cream, and delicate sweetness of agave syrup and light brown sugar.

4 cups cubed watermelon
1 sprig fresh mint, leaves picked
Juice of 1 lemon

¾ cup coconut cream
2 tablespoons agave syrup
2 tablespoons light brown sugar

IN a blender, combine the watermelon and mint and blend on high for 30 seconds. Strain the mixture through a fine-mesh sieve set over a bowl to remove the pulp.

STIR in the lemon juice, transfer to an airtight container, and refrigerate until chilled, at least 1 hour.

MEANWHILE, in a medium bowl, stir together the coconut cream, agave syrup, and brown sugar. Pour this mixture into four ice pop molds, filling them half full. Place in the freezer for 30 minutes.

CAREFULLY remove the ice pop molds from the freezer and pour the watermelon juice into the remaining half of the molds, on top of the coconut cream mixture.

FREEZE for at least 3 hours and enjoy! Don't forget to take pictures!

ACKNOWLEDGMENTS

Thank you so much to the Gallery team for all your hard work and for helping bring this book to life. Thank you to Charles Suitt of 13A for all your efforts. Thank you to Jennifer Bergstrom, Jennifer Long, and Aimée Bell; editor Aliya King Neil and assistant editor Andrew Nguyễn; Sally Marvin, Sydney Morris, Bianca Ducasse, Sienna Farris, Caroline Pallotta, and Rebecca Strobel; and to Leah Lakins for your diligence and hard work. And many, many thanks to production editor Jamie Selzer, who worked so tirelessly to bring this recipe book together.

Special thanks to my chief revenue officer, Jason Crain, my executive assistant, Keeyah Johnson, my managers Chaka Zulu and Stacey Lee Spratt, and everyone who contributed to this book. Slutty Gang, thanks for your hard work and support throughout this process. I appreciate each and every one of you.

Note: Page references in *italics* indicate photographs.

A

Almonds
    Fresh Fig Toasts, 3
Apple Butter, *156*, 157
Apples
    Apple Butter, *156*, 157
    Blueberry Sunshine Smoothie, 7
    Cranberry Relish, *160*, 161
Applesauce, replacing eggs with, xxii
Apricot Jam, 158, *159*
Artichoke Spinach Dip, 170, *171*
Arugula
    Backyard Quesadillas, 80, *81*
    Garlic Butter Tempeh Wraps, 44
Asparagus, "Bacon"-Wrapped, *78*, 79
Avocado(es)
    "Bacon" Pastry Bites, 2
    Chipotle-Stuffed, 88, *89*
    Egg Rolls, *72*, 73
    Mango Salsa, 30–32, *31*
    Parsley Moss Smoothie, 16, *17*
    Raw Vegan Chocolate Mousse, 176, *177*

B

"Bacon" (vegan)
    Avocado "Bacon" Pastry Bites, 2
    "Bacon"-Wrapped Asparagus, *78*, 79
    Brussels Rigatoni Carbonara, *122*, 123
    Cheesy Berry Poppers, *86*, 87
    Paella with Vegan Shrimp, 52, *53*
"Bacon" Broccoli Slaw, 76, *77*
"Bacon"-Wrapped Asparagus, *78*, 79
Bananas
    Berry Smoothie, *4*, 5
    Blacker Berry, Sweeter Juice, 6
    Blueberry Sunshine Smoothie, 7
    Morning Release, *14*, 15
    Parsley Moss Smoothie, 16, *17*
    replacing eggs with, xxiii
    Zucchini Cakes, 152, *153*
Barbecued "Beef" Loaf, *116*, 117
Barnwell, Crystal Shae, xviii, 88, 91
Basil
    Basic Vegan Pesto, 37
    Pineapple Salsa, *168*, 169
BBQ Tofu Bowl, 74
Bean(s)
    Backyard Quesadillas, 80, *81*
    Barbecued "Beef" Loaf, *116*, 117
    Black, and Portobello Tacos, 75
    Campfire Stew, 124, *125*

Chickpea Sunrise, 30–32, *31*
    Garbanzos Guisados (Stewed Chickpeas), 42, *43*
    Green, Mustard-Sautéed, 138, *139*
    Homemade Vegan Garlic Butter, 163
    Refried, and Portobello Soft Tacos, *82*, 83
    White, Dip, *172*, 173
Beef (vegan)
    Vegan Cheesesteak Egg Rolls, 102, *103*
"Beef" Loaf, Barbecued, *116*, 117
Beets
    Beet-tini, 28, 29
    Maple-Roasted Vegetables, 135
Berry(ies)
    Blacker, Sweeter Juice, 6
    Blueberry Sunshine Smoothie, 7
    Cranberry Relish, *160*, 161
    Poppers, Cheesy, *86*, 87
    Smoothie, *4*, 5
    Stuffed Butternut Squash, *148*, 149–50
    Sweet Bun Dessert, 184
    Zucchini Cakes, 152, *153*
Beverages
    Beet-tini, 28, 29
    Berry Smoothie, *4*, 5
    Blacker Berry, Sweeter Juice, 6
    Blueberry Sunshine Smoothie, 7
    Caramel Mocha Iced "Coffee," 8, *9*
    Habanero Margaritas, 96, 97
    Midnight Toddy, *100*, 101
    Morning Release, *14*, 15
    Parsley Moss Smoothie, 16, *17*
    Rum Punch, 45
Biscuits, Spicy Sausage Gravy and, 20–22, *21*
Blackberries
    Blacker Berry, Sweeter Juice, 6
Black-Eyed Pea(s)
    Black Pea Burgers, 84, *85*
    Stew, 120–21
Blueberry(ies)
    Berry Smoothie, *4*, 5
    Blacker Berry, Sweeter Juice, 6
    Sunshine Smoothie, 7
    Sweet Bun Dessert, 184
Bourbon
    Cauliflower, Vegan, 62–64, *63*
    Sauce, 62
Breads and toasts. *See also* Tortillas
    Avocado "Bacon" Pastry Bites, 2
    Biscuits, *21*, 22

Cheese Toasts for Onion Soup, *126*, 127
    Fresh Fig Toasts, 3
    Jalapeño Corn Bread, *136*, 137
Breakfast
    Avocado "Bacon" Pastry Bites, 2
    Berry Smoothie, *4*, 5
    Biscuits, *21*, 22
    Blacker Berry, Sweeter Juice, 6
    Blueberry Sunshine Smoothie, 7
    Caramel Mocha Iced "Coffee," 8, *9*
    Chi Chi's Vegan Churro Waffles, *10*, 11
    Fresh Fig Toasts, 3
    Garden Scramble, 12, *13*
    Morning Release, *14*, 15
    Pan-Roasted PB&J, *18*, 19
    Parsley Moss Smoothie, 16, *17*
    Spicy Sausage Gravy and Biscuits, 20–22, *21*
Broccoli
    Sesame, 58
    Slaw, "Bacon," 76, *77*
Brooks, Cierra, xix, 119
Brownies, Fudgy, 179
Brussels Rigatoni Carbonara, *122*, 123
Bun Dessert, Sweet, 184
Burgers, Black Pea, 84, *85*
Butter, Homemade Vegan Garlic, 163

C

Cabbage
    "Bacon" Broccoli Slaw, 76, *77*
    Okra Salad, *140*, 141
Campfire Stew, 124, *125*
Caramel Mocha Iced "Coffee," 8, *9*
Carob powder
    Caramel Mocha Iced "Coffee," 8, *9*
Carrots
    "Bacon" Broccoli Slaw, 76, *77*
    Barbecued "Beef" Loaf, *116*, 117
    Okra Salad, *140*, 141
    Vegan Fried Rice, 106, *107*
Cashew(s)
    Caramel Mocha Iced "Coffee," 8, *9*
    Chipotle-Stuffed Avocadoes, 88, *89*
    Creamy Pesto Mac and Cheese, *34*, 35–36
    Cup of Kelewele, 38, *39*
    Deviled N'egg, *90*, 91
    Fresh Fig Toasts, 3
    Mayo, *90*, 91
    Pesto Sauce, *34*, 35–36
    Spinach and Mushroom Alfredo, 146, *147*

Cauliflower
  Bourbon, Vegan, 62–64, *63*
  Po'boy, Island, 48, *49*
Celery
  Barbecued "Beef" Loaf, *116*, 117
  Chipotle-Stuffed Avocadoes, 88, *89*
  Deviled N'egg, *90*, 91
  Garden Scramble, 12, *13*
Cheese (vegan), xxii
  Amazing Mac 'n' Cheez, 114, *115*
  Avocado Egg Rolls, *72*, 73
  Bowl, Fondue, 162
  Brussels Rigatoni Carbonara, *122*, 123
  Cheesy Berry Poppers, *86*, 87
  Creamy Pesto Mac and, *34*, 35–36
  Eggplant Parm Marinara Fries, 129
  Elotes My Way, *40*, 41
  Fresh Fig Toasts, 3
  Fried Motz, 94
  Garden Scramble, 12, *13*
  Jalapeño Corn Bread, *136*, 137
  Sauce, 114
  Spinach Artichoke Dip, 170, *171*
  Spread, Pimento, 166
  Toasts for Onion Soup, *126*, 127
  Vegan Cheesesteak Egg Rolls, 102, *103*
  Watermelon Salad, *108*, 109
Chef El-Amin, Yusef, xv, xix, 105
Chef Nikki in the Mix, 20, 35
Chef Quan, xiv, xviii, 30
Chef Quay, xix, 98
Chia seeds
  Berry Smoothie, *4*, 5
Chi Chi's Vegan Churro Waffles, 10, 11
Chickpea flour, replacing eggs with, xxiii
Chickpea(s)
  Barbecued "Beef" Loaf, *116*, 117
  Stewed (Garbanzos Guisados), 42, *43*
  Sunrise, 30–32, *31*
Chiles
  Chipotle-Stuffed Avocadoes, 88, *89*
  Habanero Margaritas, *96*, 97
  Jalapeño Corn Bread, *136*, 137
  Spicy Garlic Eggplant, *60*, 61
Chipotle-Stuffed Avocadoes, 88, *89*
Chocolate
  Caramel Mocha Iced "Coffee," 8, *9*
  Fudgy Brownies, 179
  Mousse, Raw Vegan, 176, *177*
Churro Waffles, Chi Chi's Vegan, *10*, 11

Cinnamon
  Chi Chi's Vegan Churro Waffles, *10*, 11
  Cup of Kelewele, 38, *39*
  Midnight Toddy, *100*, 101
Cobbler, Southern Peach, 182, *183*
Cocktails
  Beet-tini, *28*, 29
  Habanero Margaritas, *96*, 97
  Midnight Toddy, *100*, 101
  Rum Punch, 45
Coconut
  Rice, 30–32, *31*
Coconut Berry Smoothie, *4*, 5
Coconut oil, xxi
"Coffee," Caramel Mocha Iced, 8, *9*
Collard Greens, Sweet and Spicy, *144*, 145
Cookies, Dee's Famous Peanut Butter, *180*, 181
Corn
  Black Pea Burgers, 84, *85*
  Elotes My Way, *40*, 41
  Jalapeño Corn Bread, *136*, 137
Cornmeal
  Black Pea Burgers, 84, *85*
  Jalapeño Corn Bread, *136*, 137
Cranberry(ies)
  Relish, *160*, 161
  Stuffed Butternut Squash, *148*, 149–50
  Zucchini Cakes, 152, *153*
Creamsicles, Watermelon, 186
Culinary Groove, *see* Chef Quay
Cup of Kelewele, 38, *39*
Curry Plantains, Raw, 56

D
Dates
  Caramel Mocha Iced "Coffee," 8, *9*
Dee's Famous Peanut Butter Cookies, *180*, 181
Desserts
  Dee's Famous Peanut Butter Cookies, *180*, 181
  Fudgy Brownies, 179
  Grilled Plums, 178
  Raw Vegan Chocolate Mousse, 176, *177*
  Southern Peach Cobbler, 182, *183*
  Sweet Bun, 184
  Sweet Potato Pudding, 185
  Watermelon Creamsicles, 186
Deviled N'egg, *90*, 91

Dips
  Fondue Cheese Bowl, 162
  Spinach Artichoke, 170, *171*
  White Bean, *172*, 173

E
Edamame
  "Bacon" Broccoli Slaw, 76, *77*
Eggplant
  Fries, 92, *93*
  Parm Marinara Fries, 129
  Spicy Garlic, *60*, 61
  Vegan Fried Fish, 66, *67*
Egg replacements, xxii–xxiii
Egg Rolls
  Avocado, *72*, 73
  Vegan Cheesesteak, 102, *103*
"Eggs," Home-Fried Potatoes with, 119
Elotes My Way, *40*, 41
Entrepreneurial wisdom, xvii–xix

F
Fajita Tacos, 33
Fig, Fresh, Toasts, 3
Fish, Vegan Fried, 66, *67*
Flaxseed
  Berry Smoothie, *4*, 5
  Caramel Mocha Iced "Coffee," 8, *9*
  Morning Release, 14, *15*
  replacing eggs with, xxii–xxiii
Fondue Cheese Bowl, 162
French-ish Onion Soup, *126*, 127–28
Fries, Eggplant Parm Marinara, 129
Fruit. *See* Berry(ies); *specific fruits*
Fruit butter. *See* Apple Butter
Fudgy Brownies, 179

G
Garbanzos Guisados (Stewed Chickpeas), 42, *43*
Garden Scramble, 12, *13*
Garlic
  Brussels Rigatoni Carbonara, *122*, 123
  Butter, Homemade Vegan, 163
  Butter Tempeh Wraps, 44
  Eggplant, Spicy, *60*, 61
  Herb Mashed Potatoes, 118
Gnocchi Florentine, 132–34, *133*
Good Ol' Southern Comfort
  Amazing Mac 'n' Cheez, 114, *115*
  Barbecued "Beef" Loaf, *116*, 117
  Black-Eyed Pea Stew, 120–21
  Brussels Rigatoni Carbonara, *122*, 123

Campfire Stew, 124, *125*
Eggplant Parm Marinara Fries, 129
French-ish Onion Soup, *126*, 127–28
Fried Green Tomatoes, 130–31
Garlic Herb Mashed Potatoes, 118
Gnocchi Florentine, 132–34, *133*
Home-Fried Potatoes with "Eggs,"
    119
Jalapeño Corn Bread, *136*, 137
Maple-Roasted Vegetables, 135
Mustard-Sautéed Green Beans, 138,
    139
Okra Salad, *140*, 141
Potato Mushroom Soup, 142, *143*
Spinach and Mushroom Alfredo,
    146, *147*
Stuffed Butternut Squash, *148*,
    149–50
Sweet and Spicy Collard Greens,
    144, 145
Zucchini Cakes, 152, *153*
Grains. *See* Cornmeal; Oats; Quinoa;
    Rice
Gravy, Spicy Sausage, and Biscuits,
    20–22, *21*
Green Beans, Mustard-Sautéed, 138,
    139
Greens. *See* Arugula; Cabbage; Collard
    Greens; Spinach; Watercress

H
Habanero Margaritas, *96*, 97
Harrell, Chris, 62
Hayes, Derrick, 102
Hearty Pepper Soup, *46*, 47
Hemp hearts
    Morning Release, *14*, 15
    Parsley Moss Smoothie, 16, *17*
Herbs
    Basic Vegan Pesto, 37
    Blacker Berry, Sweeter Juice, 6
    Parsley Moss Smoothie, 16, *17*
    Pineapple Salsa, *168*, 169
Hodge, Chris, 11

I
Island Cauliflower Po'boy, 48, *49*

J
Jalapeño Corn Bread, *136*, 137
Jam
    Apricot, 158, *159*
    Pan-Roasted PB&J, *18*, 19
Jamaican Saturdays
    Beet-tini, *28*, 29

Chickpea Sunrise, 30–32, *31*
Creamy Pesto Mac and Cheese, *34*,
    35–36
Cup of Kelewele, 38, *39*
Elotes My Way, *40*, 41
Fajita Tacos, 33
Garbanzos Guisados (Stewed
    Chickpeas), 42, *43*
Garlic Butter Tempeh Wraps, 44
Hearty Pepper Soup, *46*, 47
Island Cauliflower Po'boy, 48, *49*
Paella with Vegan Shrimp, 52, *53*
Pineapple Rice Bowl, *54*, 55
Raw Curry Plantains, 56
Roasted Purple Sweet Potatoes,
    50, 51
Rum Punch, 45
Sesame Broccoli, 58
Spicy Garlic Eggplant, *60*, 61
Vegan Bourbon Cauliflower, 62–64,
    63
Vegan Fried Fish, 66, *67*
Jicama
    Chipotle-Stuffed Avocadoes, 88, *89*
Juice, Blacker Berry, Sweeter, 6

K
Kelewele, Cup of, 38, *39*
Kick Up Rumpus
    Avocado Egg Rolls, *72*, 73
    Backyard Quesadillas, 80, *81*
    "Bacon" Broccoli Slaw, 76, *77*
    "Bacon"-Wrapped Asparagus, *78*, 79
    BBQ Tofu Bowl, 74
    Black Bean and Portobello Tacos, 75
    Black Pea Burgers, 84, *85*
    Cheesy Berry Poppers, 86, *87*
    Chipotle-Stuffed Avocadoes, 88, *89*
    Deviled N'egg, *90*, 91
    Eggplant Fries, 92, *93*
    Fried Motz, 94
    Habanero Margaritas, *96*, 97
    Midnight Toddy, *100*, 101
    Refried Bean and Portobello Soft
        Tacos, 82, 83
    Vegan Cheesesteak Egg Rolls, 102,
        103
    Vegan Fried Rice, 106, *107*
    Vegan King "Scallops," 98, *99*
    Vegan Potato Salad, *104*, 105
    Watermelon Salad, *108*, 109

L
Lucuma powder
    Parsley Moss Smoothie, 16, *17*

M
Ma'at, Tassili, 56
Mac and Cheese, Creamy Pesto, *34*,
    35–36
Mac 'n' Cheez, Amazing, 114, *115*
Mango
    Habanero Margaritas, *96*, 97
    Morning Release, *14*, 15
    Salsa, 30–32, *31*
    Watermelon Salad, *108*, 109
Maple-Roasted Vegetables, 135
Margaritas, Habanero, *96*, 97
Martinez, Luis, 42
Mayo, *90*, 91
Meat substitute. *See also* Bacon
    (vegan); Sausage (vegan)
    Hearty Pepper Soup, *46*, 47
    Vegan Cheesesteak Egg Rolls, 102,
        103
Midnight Toddy, *100*, 101
Milks, nondairy, xxii
Mint
    Blacker Berry, Sweeter Juice, 6
    Mocha Caramel Iced "Coffee," 8, *9*
    Morning Release, *14*, 15
    Moss Parsley Smoothie, 16, *17*
    Mousse, Raw Vegan Chocolate, 176,
        177
Mushroom(s)
    Black Bean and Portobello Tacos, 75
    Fajita Tacos, 33
    Garden Scramble, 12, *13*
    Gnocchi Florentine, 132–34, *133*
    Potato Soup, 142, *143*
    Refried Bean and Portobello Soft
        Tacos, 82, *83*
    Roasted Purple Sweet Potatoes,
        50, 51
    and Spinach Alfredo, 146, *147*
    Stuffed Butternut Squash, *148*,
        149–50
    Vegan King "Scallops," 98, *99*
Mustard-Sautéed Green Beans, 138,
    139

N
Nondairy milks, xxii
Nut butters, xxii
Nutritional yeast
    Amazing Mac 'n' Cheez, 114, *115*
    Cashew/Pesto Sauce, *34*, 35–36
    Cheese Sauce, 114
    Eggplant Fries, 92, *93*
    Spinach and Mushroom Alfredo,
        146, *147*

Nuts, xxii. *See also* Cashew(s)
    Cranberry Relish, *160*, 161
    Fresh Fig Toasts, 3
    Stuffed Butternut Squash, *148*,
      149–50

O

Oats
    Morning Release, *14*, 15
    Sweet Potato Pudding, 185
Oils, xxi
Okra Salad, *140*, 141
Olive oil, xxi
Onion(s)
    Garbanzos Guisados (Stewed
      Chickpeas), 42, *43*
    Maple-Roasted Vegetables, 135
    Soup, French-ish, *126*, 127–28
Oranges
    Cranberry Relish, *160*, 161
    Habanero Margaritas, *96*, 97
    Raw Vegan Chocolate Mousse, 176,
      177
    Rum Punch, 45

P

Paella with Vegan Shrimp, 52, *53*
Pantry staples, xxi–xxiii
Parsley Moss Smoothie, 16, *17*
Pasta
    Amazing Mac 'n' Cheez, 114, *115*
    Brussels Rigatoni Carbonara, *122*,
      123
    Creamy Pesto Mac and Cheese, *34*,
      35–36
    Spinach and Mushroom Alfredo,
      146, *147*
Peach Cobbler, Southern, 182, *183*
Peanut Butter
    Cookies, Dee's Famous, *180*, 181
    Pan-Roasted PB&J, *18*, 19
    Peanut Satay Dipping Sauce, 164, *165*
    Vegan Fried Rice, 106, *107*
Peas
    Black, Burgers, 84, *85*
    Black-Eyed, Stew, 120–21
    Vegan Fried Rice, 106, *107*
Pecans
    Cranberry Relish, *160*, 161
Pepper(s). *See also* Chiles
    Avocado Egg Rolls, *72*, 73
    BBQ Tofu Bowl, 74
    Black-Eyed Pea Stew, 120–21
    Black Pea Burgers, 84, *85*
    Cheesy Berry Poppers, *86*, 87

Deviled N'egg, *90*, 91
    Fajita Tacos, 33
    Mango Salsa, 30–32, *31*
    Pimento Cheese Spread, 166
    Raw Curry Plantains, 56
    Soup, Hearty, *46*, 47
Pernell, Dymetra, 181
Pesto
    Basic Vegan, 37
    Cashew, Sauce, *34*, 35–36
    Mac and Cheese, Creamy, *34*, 35–36
    Pimento Cheese Spread, 166
Pineapple
    BBQ Tofu Bowl, 74
    Beet-tini, *28*, 29
    Rice Bowl, *54*, 55
    Rum Punch, 45
    Salsa, *168*, 169
Plantains
    Chickpea Sunrise, 30–32, *31*
    Cup of Kelewele, 38, *39*
    Raw Curry, 56
Plums, Grilled, 178
Po'boy, Island Cauliflower, 48, *49*
Poppers, Cheesy Berry, *86*, 87
Potato(es). *See also* Sweet Potato(es)
    Black Bean and Portobello Tacos, 75
    Garlic Herb Mashed, 118
    Gnocchi Florentine, 132–34, *133*
    Home-Fried, with "Eggs," 119
    Maple-Roasted Vegetables, 135
    Mushroom Soup, 142, *143*
    Salad, Vegan, *104*, 105
Pudding, Sweet Potato, 185
Pumpkin seeds
    Chipotle-Stuffed Avocadoes, 88, *89*
Punch, Rum, 45

Q

Quesadillas, Backyard, 80, *81*
Quinoa
    BBQ Tofu Bowl, 74

R

Relish, Cranberry, *160*, 161
Rice
    Bowl, Pineapple, *54*, 55
    Chickpea Sunrise, 30–32, *31*
    Coconut, 30–32, *31*
    Fried, Vegan, 106, *107*
    Hearty Pepper Soup, *46*, 47
    Paella with Vegan Shrimp, 52, *53*
    Stuffed Butternut Squash, *148*,
      149–50
Rum Punch, 45

S

Safflower oil, xxi
Salads
    Okra, *140*, 141
    Potato, Vegan, *104*, 105
    Watermelon, *108*, 109
Salsa
    Mango, 30–32, *31*
    Pineapple, *168*, 169
Sandwiches
    Garlic Butter Tempeh Wraps, 44
    Island Cauliflower Po'boy, 48, *49*
    Pan-Roasted PB&J, *18*, 19
Sauces
    Bourbon, 62
    Cheese, 114
Sauces, Dipping
    for Egg Rolls, *72*, 873
    for Fried Green Tomatoes, 130–31
    Peanut Satay, 164, *165*
Sausage (vegan)
    Campfire Stew, 124, *125*
    Gravy, Spicy, and Biscuits, 20–22, *21*
    Home-Fried Potatoes with "Eggs,"
      119
    Paella with Vegan Shrimp, 52, *53*
"Scallops," Vegan King, *98*, 99
Scramble, Garden, 12, *13*
Sea moss gel
    Parsley Moss Smoothie, 16, *17*
Seeds. *See also* Flaxseed; Sesame
    seeds
    Berry Smoothie, *4*, 5
    Chipotle-Stuffed Avocadoes, 88, *89*
    Sesame Broccoli, 58
Sellers, Jeanette (aka Chef Wadada),
    16
Sesame oil, xxi
Sesame seeds
    "Bacon" Broccoli Slaw, 76, *77*
    Sesame Broccoli, 58
    Vegan Bourbon Cauliflower, 62–64,
      63
    Watermelon Salad, *108*, 109
Shrimp, Vegan, Paella with, 52, *53*
Slaw, "Bacon" Broccoli, 76, *77*
Slutty Strips
    Avocado "Bacon" Pastry Bites, 2
    "Bacon"-Wrapped Asparagus, *78*, 79
    Brussels Rigatoni Carbonara, *122*,
      123
    Cheesy Berry Poppers, *86*, 87
    Paella with Vegan Shrimp, 52, *53*
Smoothies
    Berry, *4*, 5

Blueberry Sunshine, 7
Parsley Moss, 16, *17*
Soups
Onion, French-ish, *126*, 127–28
Pepper, Hearty, *46*, 47
Potato Mushroom, 142, *143*
Spinach
Artichoke Dip, 170, *171*
BBQ Tofu Bowl, 74
Gnocchi Florentine, 132–34, *133*
Home-Fried Potatoes with "Eggs,"
119
Morning Release, *14*, 15
and Mushroom Alfredo, 146, *147*
Stuffed Butternut Squash, *148*,
149–50
Spreads
Apple Butter, *156*, 157
Apricot Jam, 158, *159*
Mayo, *90*, 91
Pimento Cheese, 166
Slutty Vegan, ix–xi, 25, 69, 111–13,
Squash
Butternut, Stuffed, *148*, 149–50
Garbanzos Guisados (Stewed
Chickpeas), 42, *43*
Zucchini Cakes, 152, *153*
Stew, Campfire, 124, *125*
Strawberries
Sweet Bun Dessert, 184
Sweet Bun Dessert, 184
Sweet Potato(es)
Backyard Quesadillas, 80, *81*
Black-Eyed Pea Stew, 120–21
Maple-Roasted Vegetables, 135
Pudding, 185
Purple, Roasted, *50*, 51

T
Tacos
Black Bean and Portobello, 75

Fajita, 33
Soft, Refried Bean and Portobello,
82, 83
Tapioca starch, replacing eggs with,
xxiii
Tea
Midnight Toddy, *100*, 101
Tempeh
"Bacon" Broccoli Slaw, 76, *77*
Wraps, Garlic Butter, 44
Toddy, Midnight, *100*, 101
Tofu
Bowl, BBQ, 74
Garden Scramble, 12, *13*
replacing eggs with, xxiii
Vegan Fried Rice, 106, *107*
Tomatoes
Avocado "Bacon" Pastry Bites, 2
"Bacon" Broccoli Slaw, 76, *77*
Campfire Stew, 124, *125*
Chipotle-Stuffed Avocadoes, 88, *89*
Deviled N'egg, *90*, 91
Dipping Sauce for Egg Rolls, *72*, 73
Garden Scramble, 12, *13*
Garlic Butter Tempeh Wraps, 44
Green, Fried, 130–31
Hearty Pepper Soup, *46*, 47
Home-Fried Potatoes with "Eggs,"
119
Okra Salad, *140*, 141
Paella with Vegan Shrimp, 52, *53*
Pineapple Rice Bowl, *54*, 55
Pineapple Salsa, *168*, 169
Vegan King "Scallops," 98, *99*
Tortillas
Backyard Quesadillas, 80, *81*
Black Bean and Portobello Tacos,
75
Fajita Tacos, 33
Refried Bean and Portobello Soft
Tacos, *82*, 83

V
Vegan lifestyle, xiii–xv
compared to vegetarian, xxv
family considerations, xxvii
FAQs, xxv–xxvii
finding vegan restaurants, xxvi
health benefits, xxv, xxvii
shopping for products, xxvi
starting on a, xxvi
Vegetables. *See also specific vegetables*
Garden Scramble, 12, *13*
Maple-Roasted, 135
Vegetarians, xxv
Vodka
Beet-tini, *28*, 29

W
Waffles, Chi Chi's Vegan Churro, *10*, 11
Walnuts
Stuffed Butternut Squash, *148*,
149–50
Watercress
Watermelon Salad, *108*, 109
Watermelon
Creamsicles, 186
Salad, *108*, 109
Wells, Erin, xiv, xix, 67
Whiskey
Midnight Toddy, *100*, 101
Williams, Suneeta (Sunni Speaks), xv,
xix, 145
Wraps, Garlic Butter Tempeh, 44

Y
Yogurt
Blueberry Sunshine Smoothie, 7
Homemade Vegan Garlic Butter,
163

Z
Zucchini Cakes, 152, *153*

the EARTH
A World to Preserve

WHITE STAR PUBLISHERS

Contents

Introduction 4

Seas 10

Mountains 74

Deserts 132

Forests 190

Glaciers 250

Savannas & Prairies 284

Fresh Water 316

Volcanoes 370

Introduction

The planet we call our own has a long history of 4.5 billion years, during which the presence of hominids dates to only 3 million years ago. The Earth was formed over a period of millions of years and continued to change even afterward. Initially with the formation of the oceans and continental crust and later with the first forms of life, it changed appearance and experienced the birth and extinction of innumerable species. It was the human species, however, that contributed the most to the transformation of the planet's environment, for better and for worse. Agriculture changed the landscape, increasingly larger cities grew where once there were only forests and marshlands, dykes and canals used to irrigate fields diverted the flow of rivers, roads and railroads cut through territories and changed their physiognomy, and the skies and the seas were traversed by routes used to transport people and merchandise. This has always been the case and we still admire the evidence left behind: the majestic monuments created by ancient civilizations such as the Egyptians, the Aztecs, and the Mayans, terraced landscapes in harmony with nature on hillsides and mountainsides, protected natural parks where there were once only swamps. Humans have spread to every part of the planet except the Antarctic and the bottom of the sea, adapting to climate and environmental conditions, creating settlements on the sides of volcanoes and in the great rainforests, surviving the rigid conditions of the Arctic, and even learning how to live in inhospitable environments like the desert.

However, there is a limit to expanding and exploiting natural resources to improve one's own life conditions. As with every species, the determining factor is demographic growth, which has gained enormous speed over the last two centuries. We reached a total population of 7.8 billion at the beginning of 2020 and an increase of 1 billion individuals every decade is predicted for the near future. This signifies a higher demand for water, food, living space, energy, and dignified living conditions. This is in addition to the effects of the industrial

• Iguazú Falls, Argentina/Brazil

revolution that began in the second half of the 18th century and is still underway, and the profit-oriented exploitation of resources that often damages the environment. Whether the problem be global warming, melting glaciers, rising sea levels, desertification, or the increase in extreme climate events, humans are at the source of it all.

The general public's attention to future threats to the planet has never been more acute. Now we know that we may never be able to reverse the damages caused in a number of biomes, particularly the oceans, glaciers, and places at risk of desertification. But we are conscious of the fact that we must stop the degradation as soon as possible if we want to re-cuperate the unique environments that are essential for the survival of many species, and we must make radical choices concerning technologies and lifestyles that have a lesser impact on the environment. These subjects have been at the heart of discussions for decades, from the international climate change conferences that opened in Rio de Janeiro in 1992 to the Paris Agreement of 2009. Agenda 2030, adopted by the United Nations in 2015, poses seventeen goals, including the fight against climate change and the conservation of our oceans, ecosystems, and biodiversity. In order to conform, the European Commission imposed a reduction in greenhouse gases by at least 55% with respect to 1990 by the year 2030.

For more than fifty years, scientists have imagined possible future scenarios as they study increasingly refined climate models that reduce the margin of error of their estimates. The factors that must be monitored are many and assembling the data gathered by numerous observers is not easy. In any case, all of them agree that global warming is increasing with respect to pre-industrial levels. According to a recent report by the Intergovernmental Panel on Climate Change, the UN's scientific forum, if drastic steps are not taken to reduce the emissions of carbon dioxide, methane, and other greenhouse gases, it will be impossible to keep temperatures from rising less than 3.6°F (2°C) by the end of the century.

Beyond institutional programs and the slowness with which they have moved until now, something is changing, particularly in the younger generation. Evidence of this change can be seen in programs like Fridays for Future, inspired by the Swedish activist Greta Thunberg. The group, who refuses to be called "environmentalists," poses urgent requests for "ecological justice," demanding that it not be the youngest generations to pay the consequences for environmental disasters and that the costs of ecological transition not fall on the shoulders of the weakest social groups, but rather on the shoulders of those who got rich with intensive exploitation. The subject of ecological justice is also part of Agenda 2030, which combines sustainable development with the fight against poverty in such a way that necessary changes will not be to the detriment of some populations and the equitable distribution of available resources is guaranteed.

Other voices join those of scientists and activists: those of writers, intellectuals, and artists who have always found inspiration in nature and who celebrate its beauty with words, music, and images.

Prestigious prizes like Wildlife Photographer of the Year and the World Nature Photography Awards have declared their purpose to be that of showing us not only the most fascinating aspects of animal life in its untamed form, plant species, and glimpses of nature in its rare beauty, but also to show us the damages created by humans and to raise public awareness and increase efforts to protect our environment. When photography is backed up with knowledge and empathy, it becomes a language that can reawaken emotions and the imagination. The photos and the quotations that accompany them in this book do just that; they help us rediscover the amazement and respect inspired by uncontaminated nature, they make us feel like small, enchanted children, and they give us a sense of belonging to this great, wonderful planet.

EARTH

Global average precipitation over land **has likely increased since 1950**, with a faster rate of increase since the 1980s.

Changes in the land biosphere since 1970 are consistent with global warming: **climate zones have shifted poleward** in both hemispheres, and the growing season has on average lengthened by up to two days per decade since the 1950s in the Northern Hemisphere extratropics.

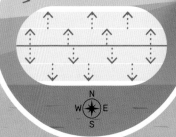

CLIMATE ZONES have shifted poleward since the 1970s.

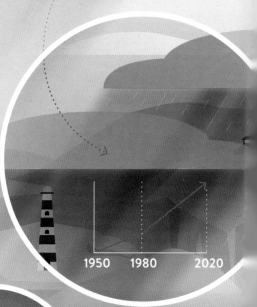

1950   1980   2020

WARMING of the open ocean surface since the 1970s.

It is virtually certain that **the global upper ocean (0–2,300 feet [0–700 m]) has warmed** since the 1970s and that **human-caused CO_2 emissions** are the main driver of **current global acidification of the open ocean surface.**

The likely range of **total human-caused global surface temperature increase** from 1850–1900 to 2010–2019 is 1.4°F (.8°C) to 2.3°F (1.3°C), with a best estimate of 1.93°F (1.07°C).

Human influence is very likely **the main driver of the global retreat of glaciers** since the 1990s and the decrease in Arctic sea ice area since 1980.

SEA LEVEL RISE between 1901 and 2018 was .66 feet (.20 m).

2006–2018
.15 inch (3.7 mm)

1901–1971
.05 inch (1.3 mm)

1971–2006
.07 inch (1.9 mm)

Sea level increased by **.66 feet (.20 m) between 1901 and 2018**. The average rate of sea level rise was .05 inch (1.3 mm) per year between 1901 and 1971. It increased to .07 inch (1.9 mm) per year between 1971 and 2006, and to .15 inch (3.7 mm) between 2006 and 2018.

Source: The Intergovernmental Panel on Climate Change (IPCC)

Seas

We don't have to engage in grand, heroic actions to participate in change. Small acts, when multiplied by millions of people, can transform the world.

| *Howard Zinn*

Seen from space, the Earth is blue. Oceans make up about 70% of its surface, and slightly less than 40% of the world's population lives near these waters. Besides offering a splendid panorama, the seas and their coasts are essential to human survival, both ecologically and economically, thanks to fishing, maritime trade, and more recently, tourism.

The immense underwater environment is unquestionably the Earth's largest biome, the only one that extends through all of the climate zones and the one that is most developed in three dimensions. The majority of seabeds are found at a depth of 3 miles (5 km). Below the surface, in the mysterious abysses, there is a wealth of life-forms that are sometimes extreme, sometimes bizarre, and often still unknown. The coastal ecosystems are also a

priceless treasure trove of nature. Where the water meets the land, environments come to life with unique structures, biodiversity, and panoramas, from the fjords of Scandinavia to the sands of the Caribbean, the Australian cliffs and the volcanic beaches of Iceland. These "border" ecosystems have immense environmental and economic value. They create natural coastal defenses that protect the inland areas, reduce the impact of coastal surges, and offer the ideal conditions for young coastal fish to nest and grow.

It is often said that we know more about the universe than we do about our planet's oceans. While this may be an exaggeration, it is undoubtedly easier to send someone into space than into the depths of the seas, where there is zero visibility, icy temperatures, and the pressure is similar to that of about fifty jumbo jets sitting on your chest. In fact, twelve humans have walked on the Moon up to now, but only three humans have gone down into the Mariana Trench. All of this makes the oceans the true frontier to explore, a world that may seem deceptively familiar but that is actually completely alien. We have already "photographed" almost the entire surface of Mars, but over 80% of the ocean floor has been mapped with a resolution of only 3 miles (5 km), which means that any object smaller than that is not on our radar. We can only imagine most of what lies beneath the surface: mountains, submerged volcanoes, coral reefs, and many forms of life.

The vital ocean spaces are much larger than any terrestrial habitat and are home to many more living beings. It is estimated that 80% of known species live underwater; 250,000 species are now described in taxonomy but the total is probably closer to 1.5 million, and many scientists agree that we will never discover them all. The variety of these ecosystems is amazing. They range from the tropical coral reefs to the arctic seas where the fish have to have an "antifreeze" element that keeps their blood from freezing. There are "fields" full of seaweed that oscillate on the seabed and the most extreme habitats in the ocean trenches where no light arrives and the only source of energy are geothermal springs.

In addition to being home to such a great concentration of life, oceans also play an essential role in regulating our planet's climate. They absorb about 30% of the carbon dioxide produced by man, mitigating its effect on global warming, and ocean currents that act as "conveyor belts" redistribute the heat absorbed in equatorial zones, gradually releasing it toward the poles.

But as precious and varied as this environment is, it is also incredibly fragile; its capacity to absorb is finite. Just like our forests, the oceans can store only so much carbon dioxide, after which they risk becoming so hot that currents would be modified and the chemical composition of the waters would change. (Oceans have become 30% more acidic over the last two centuries.) The consequent reduction in oxygen provokes the proliferation of invasive species such as algae and jellyfish, or even worse, dead zones where all forms of life disappear completely.

Rising temperatures also contribute to other, equally dangerous phenomena. Coral bleaching, for example, is caused by the loss of unicellular algae that live in symbiosis with the coral, generating vivacious colors with their photosynthetic pigments. Coral loses more than just color with the loss of the algae; it also loses its capability to survive. It is estimated that in less than thirty years, the Great Barrier Reef in Australia has lost almost half of its corals. This foreseeable tragedy risks having an even more direct effect on us: rising sea levels. With the melting of the polar caps, the volume of water in the oceans is growing rapidly, and some predict that the sea levels will increase by 39 inches (1 m) by the end of the century. An increase of just 2.7°F (1.5°C) in the average global temperature would be enough to trigger disaster. A number of studies show that by the year 2100, about 50% of vulnerable locations will experience extreme sea level events at least once a year. Many low-lying coastal areas and island archipelagos such as the Maldives and the Seychelles risk being completely submerged, and the number of people whose existence will be put at risk by the phenomenon is generally estimated at over 200 million. The mangrove forests that protect tropical and subtropical coasts are also disappearing at an alarming speed (about 2% each year). In addition to inhibiting coastal erosion and protecting the inland from extreme climate events, these aquatic forests act as a "nursery" for many marine species. They can store much more carbon than tropical forests can and their gradual disappearance will cause an estimated 240 million tons more of carbon dioxide each year (the equivalent of that produced by 50.5 million cars).

Add to this the millions of tons of plastic dumped in the oceans every year. According to many estimates, by 2050, the volume of plastic in the oceans could exceed the overall mass of their fish. Carried by currents, this trash becomes compacted and creates veritable islands, such as the Pacific Trash Vortex, which is so big that it has formed its own ecosystem–the so-called "plastisphere," a group of bacteria, viruses, and fungi that could turn out to be the cauldron of future pandemics. Waiting and hoping is not enough. The plastic is not going to disappear over time. It only breaks down into minuscule particles similar to plankton and becomes part of the marine animals' food chain, and ultimately that of humans. Approximately 80% of the plastic in our oceans comes from Asian countries, many of which, paradoxically, boast some of the world's most beautiful beaches, such as Indonesia, the Philippines, and Thailand. Most of them are developing countries where waste management is not yet able to keep up with the exponential growth of the population and the trash it produces, countries where postcard-like tropical paradises exist side by side with open-air garbage dumps on the beach or on large rivers that flow into the sea.

But it is not too late to save our planet's oceans and coasts. A number of solutions are already being studied, including the use of bacteria that feed on plastic to help clean up our waters and beaches. It is a hopeful beginning but it is not enough. Beyond that, the future of the blue ecosystem that we all depend on now depends on us.

INFOGRAPHIC

SEAS

In the last 200 years, the oceans have absorbed a third of the CO_2 produced by human activities and 90% of the extra heat trapped by the rising concentration of greenhouse gases.

90%
extra heat absorbed by the oceans

30%
CO_2 absorbed by the oceans

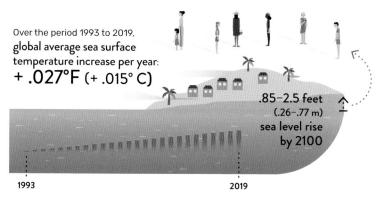

Over the period 1993 to 2019, **global average sea surface temperature increase per year:** **+ .027°F (+ .015° C)**

.85–2.5 feet (.26–.77 m) **sea level rise by 2100**

1993   2019

By 2100, sea levels will be between .85 feet (.26 m) and 2.5 feet (.77 m) higher than today. It's estimated that by 2100, **rising sea levels will threaten 200 million people** who live in low-lying coastal areas.

According to IUCN
37% endangered marine mammals

3 species critically endangered   13 species endangered   12 species vulnerable

Some species are more vulnerable to the warming of the oceans:

GRAY WHALE
Eschrichtius robustus

NORTH PACIFIC RIGHT WHALE
Eubalaena japonica

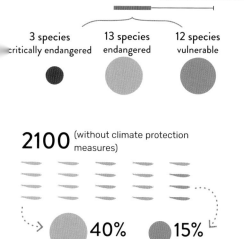

2100 (without climate protection measures)

40% in danger   **15%** vulnerable

In a scenario in which greenhouse gas emissions increase continuously, without climate protection measures, in 2100 in the ranking of the 20 most endangered marine mammal species, **40%** of the species would be in danger of extinction and **15%** of species classified as vulnerable.

Sources: The Intergovernmental Panel on Climate Change (IPCC), WWF, EU Copernicus Marine Service Information, Nature

All across the world, increasingly dangerous weather patterns and devastating storms are abruptly putting an end to the long-running debate over whether or not climate change is real. Not only is it real, it's here, and its effects are giving rise to a frighteningly new global phenomenon: the man-made natural disaster.

| *Barack Obama*

• *Gásadalur, Vágar, Faroe Islands (Denmark)*

The warnings about global warming have been extremely clear for a long time. We are facing a global climate crisis. It is deepening. We are entering a period of consequences.

| *Al Gore*

• Giant's Causeway, Northern Ireland (UK)
24–25 • Kilt Rock, Isle of Skye, Scotland (UK)

This planet came with a set of instructions, but we seem to have misplaced them. Important rules like don't poison the water, soil, or air, don't let the Earth get overcrowded, and don't touch the thermostat have been broken.

| *Paul Hawken*

• *Seven Sisters cliffs, England (UK)*

We really have the most beautiful
planet in our solar system. None other
can sustain life like we know it. None
other has blue water and white clouds
covering colorful landmasses filled with
thriving, beautiful, living things like
human beings.

| *Sunita Williams*

• Etretat cliffs, Normandy, France

Climate change is destroying our path to sustainability. Ours is a world of looming challenges and increasingly limited resources. Sustainable development offers the best chance to adjust our course.

| *Ban Ki-moon*

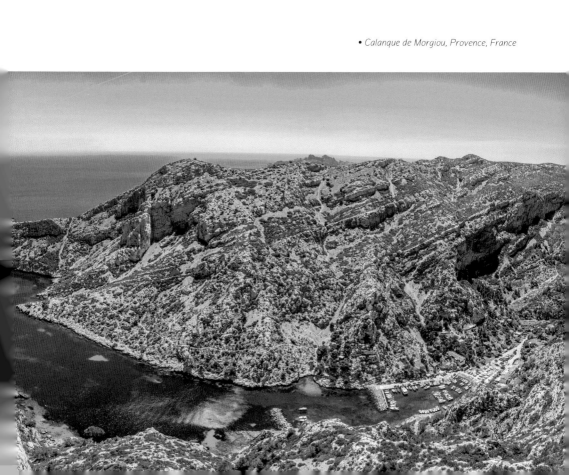

• *Calanque de Morgiou, Provence, France*

If the planet were a patient, we would have treated her long ago. You, ladies and gentlemen, have the power to put her on life support, and you must surely start the emergency procedures without further procrastination.

| *Charles, Prince of Wales*

• *Praia da Marinha, Algarve, Portugal*

When future generations judge those who came before them on environmental issues, they may conclude "they didn't know": let us not go down in history as the generations who knew, but didn't care.

| *Mikhail Gorbachev*

• Cala Pregonda, Menorca, Balearic Islands, Spain

Man, in the name of progress, is transforming the world into a stinking and poisonous place. He pollutes the air, the water, the soil, the animals . . . and himself.

| *Erich Fromm*

• *Rocky stacks of Sant'Andrea, Puglia, Italy*

The packaging for a microwavable "microwave" dinner is programmed for a shelf life of maybe six months, a cook time of two minutes and a landfill dead-time of centuries.

| *David Wann*

• Vis Island, Croatia

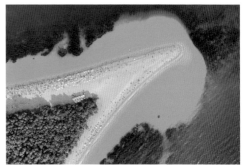

• Hvar Island, Croatia

It is unbelievably sad and ironic that
the first victims of global warming are
almost all going to come from places
that are producing virtually none of the
problem.

| *Bill McKibben*

The air, the water and the ground are free gifts to man and no one has the power to portion them out in parcels. Man must drink and breathe and walk and therefore each man has a right to his share of each.

| *James F. Cooper*

42 • Porto Katsiki Beach, Lefkada, Greece 42-43 • Navagio Beach, Zakynthos, Greece

• Skeleton Coast, Namibia 46–47 • Anse Source d'Argent, La Digue, Seychelles

It seems to me that the natural world is the greatest source of excitement; the greatest source of visual beauty; the greatest source of intellectual interest. It is the greatest source of so much in life that makes life worth living.

| *Sir David Attenborough*

I want to make it clear, if there is ever
a conflict between environmental quality
and economic growth, I will go for
beauty, clean air, water, and landscape.

| *Jimmy Carter*

The climate bill has finally come due.
Who will pay? Right now it is being paid
by the smallest and most vulnerable.
We see a small toll exacted every day
as our shorelines are surely eroded.
Small island communities are among
the first to pay the price of climate
change but no one will escape forever.

| *Baron Waqa*

• *Maldives*

You cannot protect the environment unless you empower people, you inform them, and you help them understand that these resources are their own, that they must protect them.

| *Wangari Maathai*

Phang Nga Bay, Thailand

If you really think that the environment is less important than the economy, try holding your breath while you count your money.

| *Guy McPherson*

Earth and sky, woods and fields, lakes and rivers, the mountain and the sea, are excellent schoolmasters, and teach some of us more that what we could learn from books.

| *John Lubbock*

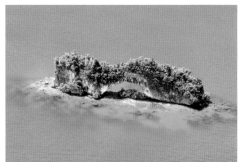

• *Rock Islands, Palau*

Preservation of the environment,
promotion of sustainable development
and particular attention to climate
change are matters of grave concern
for the entire human family.

| *Pope Benedict XVI*

• Twelve Apostles, Victoria, Australia 62–63 • Bora Bora, French Polynesia 64–65 • Na Pali Coast, Kauai, Hawaii (USA)

• Great Barrier Reef, Australia

By polluting the oceans, not mitigating carbon dioxide emissions and destroying our biodiversity, we are killing our planet. Let us face it, there is no planet B.

| *Emmanuel Macron*

• *Big Sur, California (USA)*

• *Bandon Beach, Oregon (USA)*

The language "it's too late" is very unsuitable for most environmental issues. It's too late for the dodo and for people who've starved to death already, but it's not too late to prevent an even bigger crisis. The sooner we act on the environment, the better.

| *Jeremy Grantham*

• *Cabo San Lucas, Baja California, Mexico*

Ten percent of the big fish still remain. There are still some blue whales. There are still some krill in Antarctica. There are a few oysters in Chesapeake Bay. Half the coral reefs are still in pretty good shape, a jeweled belt around the middle of the planet. There's still time, but not a lot, to turn things around.

| *Sylvia Earle*

• *Martinique (France)*

I think the environment should be put in the category of our national security. Defense of our resources is just as important as defense abroad. Otherwise what is there to defend?

| *Robert Redford*

Try and leave this world a little better
than you found it, and when your turn
comes to die, you can die happy in feeling
that at any rate, you have not wasted
your time but have done your best.

| *Robert Baden-Powell*

Mountains

Though men now possess the power
to dominate and exploit every corner
of the natural world, nothing in that
fact implies that they have the right
or the need to do so.

| *Edward Abbey*

In our eyes, mountains may look like they are always immobile and immutable, but in reality, they are the most ancient proof of the gradual but enormous changes that our planet has undergone in its millions of years of history. It is hard to imagine that in other geological eras, where majestic mountain chains now stand, there were tropical lagoons that left behind fossils of fish and other aquatic animals set in stone, or that the mountains of the "youngest" chains, the Alps and the Himalayas, are still developing.

Orogeny, or the process in which mountains form, can depend on a variety of factors, one of the most important of which, continental drift, is a phenomenon first identified by the geologist Alfred Wegener in 1912. Wegener perceived that the Earth's crust floated on a denser,

more fluid layer that, when heated by the Earth's inner core, generated movements that transported chunks of the lighter, thinner pieces of the superficial crust. Fractures and separations created chasms and valleys while, at the same time, the collision between chunks of landmass resulted in the creation of mountainous elevations. This is what happened in the case of the Himalayas, which have the planet's highest peaks, as well as with the Alps and the Apennines in Europe. Other mountains are volcanic, formed by the stratified lava of ancient eruptions. Characterized by their unique conic shape, the peaks of Kilimanjaro in Tanzania, of Fuji in Japan, and of Mauna Loa in Hawaii are easily recognizable.

Mountains have a variety of shapes, mineral compositions, and heights, and are one of the geographic features that most define a region. They create majestic landscapes like the surreal ones of Mount Danxia in China, the rainbow waves of Mount Vinicunca in Peru, and the pink shades cast by the mountains in the Italian Dolomites. Some rise up solitary and pointed, like the Cerro Torre in Argentina, or tower overhead, flat and massive like Venezuela's Roraima with its thousands of waterfalls.

But mountains are more than the spectacular expression of what happens in the Earth's core. They are extremely important "strongboxes" of fresh water that hold more ice and snow in their peaks than anywhere else on the planet, with the exception of the poles. There are over 200,000 glaciers, snow deposits, and high elevation lakes in the world, and all together, mountains hold almost half of all the fresh water used by man. At the most impervious altitudes, rock interacts with water in both its solid and liquid forms. Glaciers dig into the mountain to form lakes while springs at high elevations give origin to rivers that flow to the valleys below, sometimes for thousands of miles, taking water to human settlements and the cultivations that are the basis of our survival. For millennia, man knew how to live in symbiosis with mountains and adapt to specific conditions in order to have the necessary resources to survive.

Yet, in recent years, even the least accessible peaks are deteriorating under the weight of pollution and climate change. Many glaciers are experiencing the phenomenon known as "black carbon," a deposit of dust resulting from human activity and fires (some of which burned miles away) that makes the ice melt faster. Black carbon, microplastics, and even nuclear waste found in the glaciers are a glaring sign of the impact of human activity on the environment, but global warming is also responsible. The duration of the snow mantle is decreasing in almost all the regions of the world, particularly at lower elevations, as are the surface and volume of the world's glaciers. It is estimated that in the last 100 years (at a much higher speed in the last 30), alpine glaciers have shrunk by more than 50%, and that if the trend is not stopped, they could disappear almost completely before the next century.

It is more than an immeasurable loss for the natural environment; it is a concrete danger to human survival. The progressive, constant reduction of glaciers is responsible for the creation of ephemeral lakes that can flood and flow into the valleys causing destruction and loss of life. It also causes extreme changes in the water levels of rivers with alternating periods of low water and violent flooding that can provoke lethal damages to the countries whose economies depend on those rivers. One example is India, where, according to a UN report, the glaciers that feed the Ganges River could melt by 2030, but the phenomenon also affects many European rivers that are fundamental for navigation and to power hydroelectric plants.

The alarm bells are already ringing. Even though it may be impossible to recuperate what has already been lost, it is imperative that we stop this race toward disaster as soon as possible.

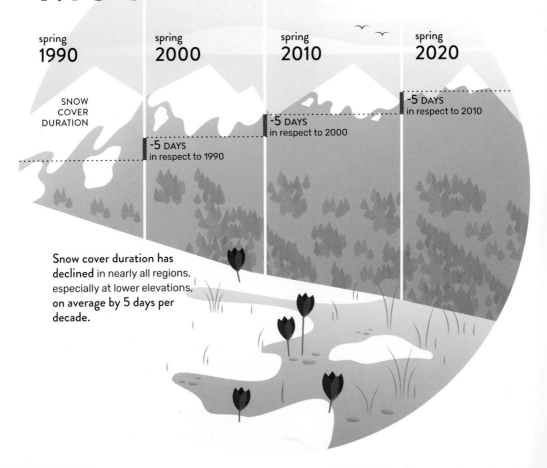

MOUNTAINS

spring
1990

spring
2000

spring
2010

spring
2020

SNOW
COVER
DURATION

-5 DAYS
in respect to 1990

-5 DAYS
in respect to 2000

-5 DAYS
in respect to 2010

Snow cover duration has **declined** in nearly all regions, especially at lower elevations, on average by 5 days per decade.

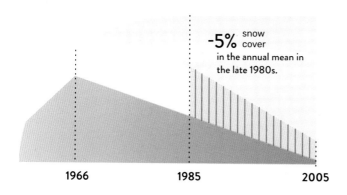

-5% snow cover in the annual mean in the late 1980s.

1966   1985   2005

Northern Hemisphere snow cover observed by satellite over the **1966 to 2005** period decreased in every month (except November and December), with a stepwise **drop of 5%** in the annual mean in the late 1980s.

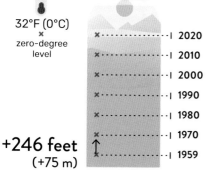

32°F (0°C)
× zero-degree level

+246 feet (+75 m)

× | 2020
× | 2010
× | 2000
× | 1990
× | 1980
× | 1970
× | 1959

In the Alpine region, **the zero-degree level** in summer has risen about **246 feet (75 m)** per decade since 1959.

GLACIERS' MASS LOSS
2–3% per year

ALPINE GLACIER

Alpine glaciers have been receding since the 1980s. In terms of **mass**, the current **loss** rate for a sample of eight Alpine glaciers is estimated to be **2–3% per year**.

2.2 lbs (1 kg) of CO_2 emitted costs 33 lbs (15 kg) of glacier ice. In the long run, **1,640 feet (500 m) driven by car** with a mid-range vehicle will **cost 2.2 lbs (1 kg) of glacier ice**.

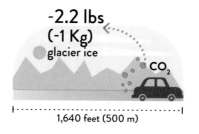

-2.2 lbs (-1 Kg) glacier ice

CO_2

1,640 feet (500 m)

Sources: ICPP, Nature Climate Change, Centre for Development and Environment (CDE), Swiss Agency for Development and Cooperation (SDC), Geographica Bernensia

Is wellbeing only economic growth?
Only salaries? Or is wellbeing also
being able to breathe clean air
and drink clean water?

| Frans Timmermans

We realize the indivisibility of the Earth—its soil, mountains, rivers, forests, climate, plants, and animals—and respect it collectively not only as a useful servant but as a living being, vastly less alive than ourselves in degree, but vastly greater than ourselves in time and space—a being that was old when the morning stars sang together, and when the last of us has been gathered unto his fathers, will still be young.

| *Aldo Leopold*

• Monte Perdido, Spain

Mountains know secrets we need to learn. That might take time, it might be hard, but if you just hold on long enough, you will find the strength to rise up.

| *Tyler Knott Gregson*

88-89 • Mont Blanc Massif, Italy/France 89 • Les Grandes Joresses, Mont Blanc Massif, France

Climb the mountain not to plant your flag, but to embrace the challenge, enjoy the air and behold the view. Climb it so you can see the world, not so the world can see you.

| *David McCullough Jr.*

The choice to "do nothing" in response to the mounting evidence is actually a choice to continue and even accelerate the reckless environmental destruction that is creating the catastrophe at hand.

| *Al Gore*

90 • Aiguille du Midi, Mont Blanc Massif, France 91 • Dent du Géant, Mont Blanc Massif, Italy/France

When you stand at the bottom of the mountain and look up at the mountaintop, the path looks hard and stony, and the top is obscured by clouds. But when you reach the top and you look down, you realize that there are a thousand paths that could have brought you to that place.

| *Roz Savage*

• *Mont Blanc, Italy/France*

In the 19th century, we devoted our best minds to exploring nature. In the 20th century, we devoted ourselves to controlling and harnessing it. In the 21st century, we must devote ourselves to restoring it.

| *Stephen Ambrose*

• *Matterhorn, Italy/Switzerland*

Thank goodness for the first snow, it
is a reminder—no matter how old you
became and how much you'd seen,
things could still be new if you were
willing to believe they still mattered.

| *Candace Bushnell*

There's no glory in climbing a mountain
if all you want to do is to get to the top.
It's experiencing the climb itself—in all
its moments of revelation, heartbreak,
and fatigue—that has to be the goal.

| *Karyn Kusama*

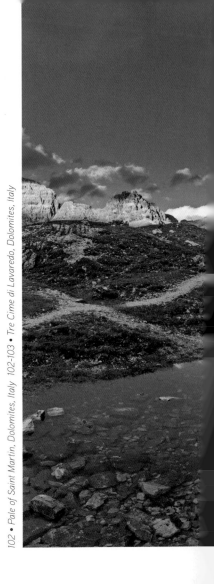

Do we have to wait until a disaster overwhelms us before we make the radical changes necessary to protect our world for future generations? That is the vital challenge of sustainable development. If we act now there is much that can be saved which will otherwise disappear forever.

| *John Gummer*

• *Marmolada, Dolomites, Italy*

If people destroy something replaceable made by mankind, they are called vandals; if they destroy something irreplaceable made by God, they are called developers.

| *Joseph Wood Krutch*

Mountains are not stadiums where
I satisfy my ambition to achieve, they
are the cathedrals where I practice
my religion.

| *Anatoli Boukreev*

• K2, Pakistan/China

• *Mount Kailash, China*

With time environmental issues got much more complicated. It is pretty easy, if you know what you are doing, to stop a company from pouring poison into a lake where kids swim. It is much harder to address all the myriad greenhouse gases emitted by different sources—from petrochemical refineries to hundreds of millions of peasants cutting down trees for their incredibly inefficient cook stoves.

| *Denis Hayes*

Sooner or later, we will have to recognise that the Earth has rights, too, to live without pollution. What mankind must know is that human beings cannot live without Mother Earth, but the planet can live without humans.

| *Evo Morales*

• *Mount Everest, Changtse, and Nuptse, Nepal/China*
116–117 • Mount Everest, Nepal/China

The Earth, the air, the land, and the water are not an inheritance from our forefathers but on loan from our children. So we have to hand over to them at least as it was handed over to us.

| *Gandhi*

• *Sagarmatha National Park, Nepal*

There is no such sense of solitude
as that which we experience upon
the silent and vast elevations of great
mountains. Lifted high above the level
of human sounds and habitations,
among the wild expanses and colossal
features of Nature, we are thrilled in
our loneliness with a strange fear and
elation—an ascent above the reach of
life's expectations or companionship,
and the tremblings of a wild and
undefined misgivings.

| *J. Sheridan Le Fanu*

• *Aoraki/Mount Cook, New Zealand*

Instead of controlling the environment for the benefit of the population, perhaps we should control the population to ensure the survival of our environment.

| *Sir David Attenborough*

Castle Mountain, Rocky Mountains, Canada

Every time I have some moment
on a seashore, or in the mountains,
or sometimes in a quiet forest, I think
this is why the environment has
to be preserved.

| *Bill Bradley*

126 • *El Capitan, Yosemite National Park, California (USA)*
127 • *Half Dome, Yosemite National Park, California (USA)*

If you are faced with a mountain, you have several options. You can climb it and cross to the other side. You can go around it. You can dig under it. You can fly over it. You can blow it up. You can ignore it and pretend it's not there. You can turn around and go back the way you came. Or you can stay on the mountain and make it your home.

| *Vera Nazarian*

• Alpamayo, Peru 130–131 • Torres Del Paine, Chile

Deserts

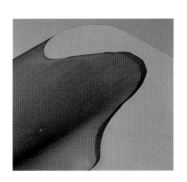

Climate change is real. It is happening right now, it is the most urgent threat facing our entire species and we need to work collectively together and stop procrastinating.

| *Leonardo DiCaprio*

The Latin verb *deserere* means "to abandon"; its past participle is *desertum*, and, in fact, in our imagination, we immediately associate the word "desert" with a territory so inhospitable that it has to be abandoned, a territory where nothing and no one can survive. But what exactly is a desert? Beyond the folkloristic image of white sand dunes and caravans of camels and men in blue turbans, deserts are one of the most diverse environments imaginable. They account for approximately 30% of the Earth's dry land surface and extend beyond the planet's hottest areas. Some deserts are scorching and others are freezing, some are along the coasts and others are far from the oceans. There are salt deserts, sand deserts, gravelly or rocky deserts, and even deserts covered by the eternal ice of the poles. In reality, only one

feature is common to these disparate territories—the scarceness of rain. A territory can only be defined as desert if the precipitation there is less than 9.8 inches per year (250 mm/y), a quantity that evaporates almost immediately. In fact, the desert is the only biome on Earth that may not see rain for entire years.

These ecosystems are made of extremes. The temperatures there range from over 122°F (50°C) in the hot deserts during summer to under -40°F (-40°C) in the cold deserts during winter, and even in the same desert, the temperature range is disconcerting: on a typical day in the Sahara, temperatures can easily go from 100°F (38°C) at midday to 41°F (5°C) at midnight. This phenomenon is caused by a number of factors. The most important is the lack of humidity in the air, which grows red-hot with the sun during the day but is unable to hold heat during the night. In addition, deserts have no seas or lakes that would help mitigate the climate by absorbing and gradually releasing heat from the ground.

The scarcity of water in the desert makes the ground arid and limits vegetation, but even here, when conditions are right, life flourishes. For example, in the Atacama Desert, between Chile and Peru, the rare autumn rains that fall once every 5–7 years transform the desert's lunar landscape into an alpine meadow covered by spectacular florescence. This phenomenon, which lasts for only a few weeks, also happens in other deserts around the world, including the Gobi in Asia and the Namaqualand in Africa. Even under normal conditions, deserts are not as "deserted" as you may think. In the oases of the Maghreb, palm and tamarind trees grow, and in the sunny expanses in Mexico, cacti and agave plants flourish. These plants have adapted to extremely harsh conditions. They are covered with little hairs that hold humidity and their leaves have become spines or prickles to reduce transpiration. They have developed long roots that can "hunt" for water deep in the earth, and they have developed reserve fibers where they hold the humidity they absorb from the rare rains (which is why we call them succulents).

Desert fauna has also had to find creative means to survive. Most of them only come out at night, they drink rarely, and they have developed unconventional strategies to conserve liquids (like the humps of camels). Generally speaking, deserts have a low level of biodiversity. This means that their vast surfaces are home to only a few animal and plant species, each of which has a reduced number of individuals, including humans. While they may not be completely uninhabited, deserts do not have the conditions necessary to develop large groups of resident populations, except in proximity of the oases. The human population is made up almost entirely of nomadic peoples, such as the Tuareg, who still perpetuate their traditional lifestyles.

But the desert is different from all the other biomes for another reason as well: it is the only one that is not threatened. This may sound like good news, but in reality, it is not particularly. The deserts' good health is allowing them to expand more and more and erode the vital space of other ecosystems. Drought and desertification have become the number one problem in many areas of the world. According to the UN Convention to Combat Desertification, 25% of the Earth's surface is near destruction or already destroyed, with peaks of 60% recorded in Africa. Some predictions estimate that by 2050, desertification will have claimed half of the agricultural land in South Africa. In less than 10 years, half of humanity will probably live in areas at high risk of drought, and the tendency toward aridity is not even sparing the "rich" countries in temperate climate zones. Poor land management, deforesting, and the exploitation of intensive agriculture have had a detrimental effect on the planet's delicate hydrological equilibrium. We need to take steps immediately if we do not want the Earth to become one huge desert.

DESERTS

Globally, a total area of land half of the size of the European Union (1.61 million mi² [4.18 million km²]) is degraded annually, with Africa and Asia being the most affected.

46,000 mi²
(120,000 km²)
Desertification and drought

1,610,000 mi²
(4,180,000 km²)
Soil degradation

Similarly, 30 million acres (12 million hectares) of land (an area the size of Benin) are lost every year to desertification and drought alone.

Water scarcity affects between 1–2 billion people, most of whom live in drylands. Under the climate change scenario, nearly half of the world's population in 2030 will be living in areas of high water stress.

low water stress

high water stress

1 billion people

2020
1–2 billion people live in drylands.

2030
about 4 billion people will be living under high water stress.

about 7,500,000,000 world population

WEST AFRICA
The rainfall decline over tropical West Africa exceeds -.04 inch (-1.0 mm) per day per century.

+11%–18%
Sahara Desert's area over the twentieth century.

-10%/-25%
decline in seasonal rainfall over the course of the twentieth century.

SAHARA DESERT
The Sahara Desert has expanded significantly over the twentieth century, by 11%–18% depending on the season and by 10% when defined using annual rainfall.

Sources: United Nations Convention to Combat Desertification, World Water Development Report, American Meteorological Society, Joint Research Centre (JRC)

For over three decades, the international community has grappled with drought impacts and their mitigation. In most cases, the response is too late. Investing in our resilience today costs a fraction of the relief price we will pay tomorrow, and its benefits are worth far more. Becoming a drought-resilient global society is not only possible and affordable, it must be our first and only option.

| *Luc Gnacadja*

140–141 • *Sahara Desert, Morocco* • *Ziz Oasis, Morocco*

• Tassili n'Ajjer, Algeria

Climate change is the greatest
threat to humanity, perhaps ever.
Global temperatures are rising
at an unprecedented rate,
causing drought and forest fires
and impacting human health.

| *Cary Kennedy*

• Hoggar Mountains, Algeria

144

I think we are bound to, and by, nature.
We may want to deny this connection
and try to believe we control the
external world, but every time there's
a snowstorm or drought, we know our
fate is tied to the world around us.

| *Alice Hoffman*

Nowhere is this challenge more critical—and the need for action more pressing —than in the Horn of Africa. From Kenya to Ethiopia, Djibouti to Somalia, the devastating consequences of drought, desertification and land degradation are playing out before our eyes.

| *Rajiv Shah*

• *Sahara Desert, Libya*

Erosion, desertification, and pollution have become our lot. It is a weird form of suicide, for we are bleeding our planet to death.

| *Gerald Durrell*

The planet has a fever. If your baby has a fever, you go to the doctor. If the doctor says you need to intervene here, you don't say, "Well, I read a science fiction novel that told me it's not a problem." You take action.

| *Al Gore*

• White Desert, Egypt 154–155 • Sinai Desert, Egypt

The desert is so vast that no one can know it all. Men go out into the desert, and they are like ships at sea; no one knows when they will return.

| *Jean-Marie Gustave Le Clézio*

• Deadvlei, Namibia

You don't know how to bring salmon back up a dead stream. You don't know how to bring back an animal now extinct. And you can't bring back forests that once grew where there is now desert. If you don't know how to fix it, please stop breaking it!

| *Severn Cullis-Suzuki*

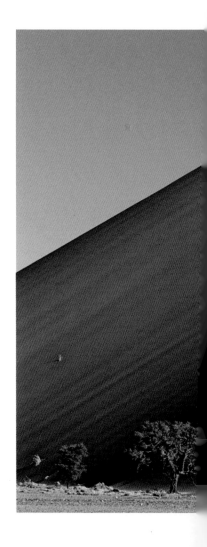

Sossusvlei, Namibia

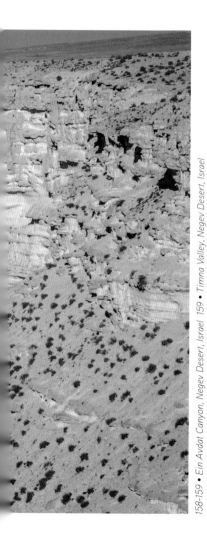

158-159 • Ein Avdat Canyon, Negev Desert, Israel 159 • Timna Valley, Negev Desert, Israel

If not prevented, desertification of the world can one day make the camels as the best and the sole cars of our civilization!

| *Mehmet Murat İldan*

The pace of global warming is accelerating and the scale of the impact is devastating. The time for action is limited—we are approaching a tipping point beyond which the opportunity to reverse the damage of carbon dioxide emissions will disappear.

| *Eliot Spitzer*

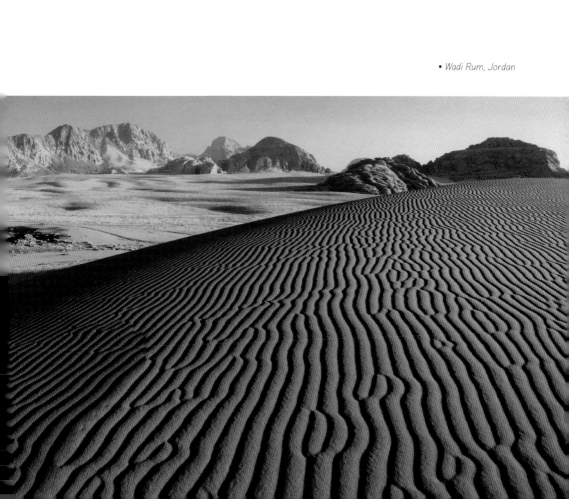

• Wadi Rum, Jordan

Animal agriculture makes a 40%
greater contribution to global warming
than all transportation in the world
combined; it is the number one cause
of climate change.

| *Jonathan Safran Foer*

Nature doesn't need people—people need nature; nature would survive the extinction of the human being and go on just fine, but human culture, human beings, cannot survive without nature.

| *Harrison Ford*

• *Empty Quarter, Oman*

Shame on us if 100 years from now our grandchildren are living on a planet that has been irreparably damaged by global warming, and they ask, "How could those who came before us, who saw this coming, have let this happen?"

| *Joe Lieberman*

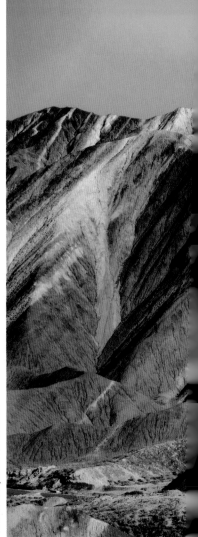

• *Danxia Landform, Gansu, China*

• Tsagaan Suvarga, Mongolia

• Gobi Desert, Mongolia

One can see from space how the human race has changed the Earth. Nearly all of the available land has been cleared of forest and is now used for agriculture or urban development. The polar icecaps are shrinking and the desert areas are increasing. At night, the Earth is no longer dark, but large areas are lit up. All of this is evidence that human exploitation of the planet is reaching a critical limit.

| *Stephen Hawking*

• Kata Tjuta, Northern Territory, Australia

• Uluru, Northern Territory, Australia

We have probed the Earth, excavated it, burned it, ripped things from it, buried things in it. That does not fit my definition of a good tenant. If we were here on a month-to-month basis, we would have been evicted long ago.

| *Rose Bird*

• *Death Valley National Park, California (USA)*

• *Death Valley National Park, California (USA)*

When the Earth is sick and polluted, human health is impossible. To heal ourselves we must heal our planet, and to heal our planet we must heal ourselves.

| *Bobby McLeod*

I don't see the desert as barren at all;
I see it as full and ripe. It doesn't need
to be flattered with rain. It certainly
needs rain, but it does with what it has,
and creates amazing beauty.

| *Joy Harjo*

• Mojave Desert, California (USA)

Both degradation and desertification are the most critical environmental issues of our time. They are linked to food security, poverty, urbanization, climate change and biodiversity loss.

| *Edna Molewa*

• *The Wave, Vermillion Cliffs, Arizona (USA)*

I think we should all be more concerned about the environment and the effects of global warming. It will be pointless to talk about all the issues that divide us when it's 300 degrees outside.

| *Don Cheadle*

• *Canyonlands National Park, Utah (USA)*

• Arches National Park, Utah (USA)

A more robust approach to global warming is needed if we are to avoid catastrophe. Unlike the recent financial crisis, there is no bailout option for the Earth's climate.

| *José Ángel Gurría*

• Bryce Canyon National Park, Utah (USA)

Those who dwell among the beauties
and mysteries of the Earth are never
alone or weary of life. The more clearly
we can focus our attention on the
wonders and realities of the universe,
the less taste we shall have
for destruction.

| *Rachel Carson*

• *Monument Valley, Arizona/Utah (USA)*

White Sands, New Mexico (USA)

We already have the statistics for the
future: the growth percentages of
pollution, overpopulation, desertification.
The future is already in place.

| *Günter Grass*

White Sands, New Mexico (USA) 188-189 • Salar de Uyuni, Bolivia

Mother Nature is a lot like your body. If your temperature goes from 98.6 to 100.6, you don't feel so good. If it goes from 100.6 to 102.6, well, you call the doctor. If it goes from 102.6 to 104.6, you're in the emergency room at a hospital. The same with Mother Nature—small changes in global average temperatures have a huge climate effect.

| *Thomas Friedman*

Forests

What we are doing to the forests

of the world is but a mirror

reflection of what we are doing to

ourselves and to one another.

| *Gandhi*

When we are asked to imagine an uncontaminated natural environment, the first one that comes to mind is usually a forest. In our imagination, forests have played a special role since the beginning of time, whether they be a familiar kind of local forest, perhaps crowned by the colors of fall, or a tangle of leaves and lianas in the Amazon rainforest, or maybe even a frozen expanse of fir trees deep in Alaska. They represent the beginning of the history of humans and the frontier between civilization and untamed nature that we find in fairy tales, myths, and legends in almost every culture. For thousands of years, they have contributed to the survival of hunter-gatherer populations and have been a favorite place to hold magic rituals and initiation rites. Later, the forest became the realm of the unknown in the collective

  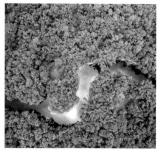

subconscious, a place to venture into only at your own risk and peril, and never after dark, when it became a lair of witches and wolves, of hybrid monstrous creatures, or more commonly, of criminals, thieves, and anyone else who had problems with the law or with civil society. Then, in modern times, its halo of romanticism and unsettling mystery was swept away and the forest became simply one more land to be conquered and exploited. It may seem like today's world can do without forests and that the cities we live in are increasingly "sterilized" with asphalt and concrete, but in reality, the forests are more essential to our survival than ever before. They cover approximately a third of the planet's land surface, and regardless of the climate zone in which they are located, they are the "lungs" of the Earth. Through photosynthesis, they contribute to the production of oxygen and help control levels of carbon dioxide in the atmosphere. They help to regulate climate and temperature, to limit land erosion, to purify the air we breathe, and to hold humidity in the atmosphere. In addition, forests are invaluable sanctuaries of biodiversity. They are home to countless species of plants and animals (according to some estimates, about 80% of the planet's species), many of which have yet to be discovered, as well as to the dozens of indigenous populations that continue to live in total symbiosis with nature. Nevertheless, this extraordinary natural heritage is in more danger than it ever has been. It is estimated that approximately 1.6 million square miles (420 M ha) of forest have been destroyed since 1990 and even though deforestation has decreased slightly over the last three decades, the world's major forests (those never exploited by humans), have shrunk by more than 309,000 square miles (80 M ha). Early statistics indicate that 2020 was a particularly bad year. In twelve months, over 46,300 square miles (12 M ha) of tropical forests were destroyed, including 16,200 square miles (4.2 M ha) of rainforest that had been previously untouched (an increase of 12% compared to 2019). The World Resources Institute reports that this loss has caused an increase in carbon dioxide emissions of 2.64 million tons, almost double of that currently produced by all of the cars circulating in the United States.

The traditional "natural" threats to forests, such as spontaneous fires, hurricanes, drought, frost, and parasite infestations, have given way to the threat posed by humans: in part, the deforestation to obtain wood, but even more importantly, the need to continually create new spaces for agriculture and intensive animal farming. The countries where this occurs most often are those in tropical zones, which happen to be where the most biodiverse forests are found, such as Brazil, the Congo, and the countries in Southeast Asia. Here, growing quantities of forest are cut down or burned every year to make way for grazing lands and large plantations of soy, coffee, cacao, and tropical fruit destined to meet the needs of an increasingly global, consumeristic market, a market that is jeopardizing the future of humanity and the planet in the name of profit.

But it is not too late to intervene. The situation is undoubtedly serious, but there have been some signs of countertrends. In the temperate climate zones, particularly in China, Australia, India, and Europe, forests are regaining ground and are showing a constant growth from year to year. This demonstrates that the conscious, respectful use of resources can help battle deforestation and climate change. We are still far from having a solution, but at least we know that a different future is possible.

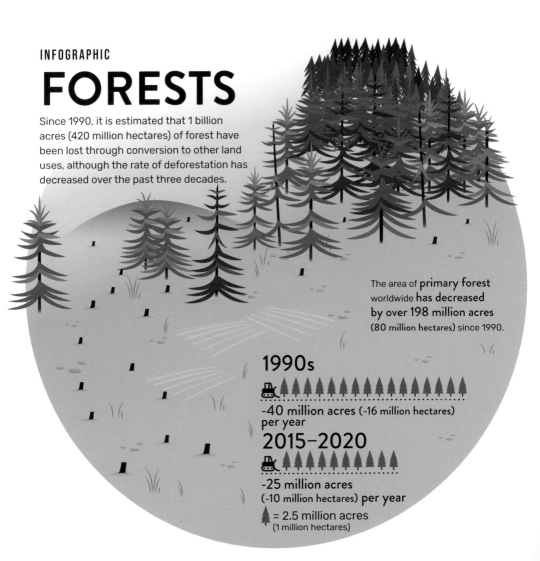

INFOGRAPHIC

FORESTS

Since 1990, it is estimated that 1 billion acres (420 million hectares) of forest have been lost through conversion to other land uses, although the rate of deforestation has decreased over the past three decades.

The area of **primary forest** worldwide **has decreased by over 198 million acres** (80 million hectares) since 1990.

1990s

-40 million acres (-16 million hectares) per year

2015–2020

-25 million acres (-10 million hectares) **per year**

= 2.5 million acres (1 million hectares)

30%

of the globe's 60,000 tree species–17,500 species– **is currently at risk of extinction.**

25%

Indonesia and Malaysia are both among the top 5 biodiverse countries in the world with 5,716 and 5,422 tree species respectively. Nearly 25% of these are threatened.

20%

The country with the single largest number of threatened tree species is **Brazil**. The Latin American nation counts 8,847 tree species–the highest number in the world–but about a fifth (1,788) are threatened.

The **top three threats facing tree species** are crop production, timber logging, and livestock farming.

Climate change and extreme weather are emerging threats.

Sources: Botanic Gardens Conservation International (BGCI), FAO

It is imperative to maintain portions
of the wilderness untouched so that
a tree will rot where it falls, a waterfall
will pour its curve without generating
electricity, a trumpeter swan may float
on uncontaminated water.

| *Bernard DeVoto*

• *Irati Forest, Spain*

Trees are the best monuments that
a man can erect to his own memory.
They speak his praises without flattery,
and they are blessings to children
yet unborn.

| *Earl of Orrery*

A nation that destroys its soils destroys itself. Forests are the lungs of our land, purifying the air and giving fresh strength to our people.

| *Franklin D. Roosevelt*

202 • Bamselitjernet Lake, Norway
203 • Oulanka National Park, Finland

When the last tree is cut, the last fish
is caught, and the last river is polluted;
when to breathe the air is sickening,
you will realize, too late, that wealth
is not in bank accounts and that
you can't eat money.

| *Alanis Obomsawin*

I could survive the disappearance of all
the cathedrals in the world, but I could
never survive the disappearance of
the woods I see every morning from
my window.

| *Ermanno Olmi*

When we plant trees, we are doing
what we can to make our planet a more
wholesome and happier dwelling place
for those who come after us, if not for
ourselves.

| *Oliver Wendell Holmes Jr.*

• Black Forest, Germany •

210-211 • *Bialowieza Forest, Poland/Belarus* 211 • *European bison, Bialowieza Forest, Poland/Belarus*

Unless we change our food choices,
nothing else matters. Because it is meat
that is destroying most of our forests.
It is meat that pollutes the waters.
So, it's the first choice for anybody who
wants to save the Earth.

| *Maneka Gandhi*

Gorillas are brave and loyal. They help
each other, they rival elephants
as parents and whales for gentleness,
they play and have humor and they harm
nothing, they are what we should be.
I don't know if we'll ever get there.

| *Pat Derby*

• *Bwindi Impenetrable National Park, Uganda*

• *Tsingy de Bemaraha, Madagascar*

We are consuming our forests three times faster than they are being reproduced. Some of the richest timber lands of this continent have already been destroyed, and not replaced, and other vast areas are on the verge of destruction. Yet forests, unlike mines, can be so handled as to yield the best results of use, without exhaustion, just like grain fields.

| *Theodore Roosevelt*

217

• Spotted deer, Sundarbans, Bangladesh/India

• Bengal tiger, Sundarbans, Bangladesh/India

There are six billion egos living on this planet. Can you not see why the world is in such a sorry state? Can you not see why we are destroying Heaven on Earth for our own short-term gain? Can you not see why the tiger and the gorilla are facing extinction, along with countless other species?

| *Mary Bruggeman*

Animals are, like us, endangered species on an endangered planet, and we are the ones who are endangering them, it, and ourselves. They are innocent sufferers in a hell of our making.

| *Jeffrey Moussaieff Masson*

Never say there is nothing beautiful in
the world anymore. There is always
something to make you wonder in the
shape of a tree, the trembling of a leaf.

| *Albert Schweitzer*

Every tree in the forest has a story to tell. Some of them were burnt but they endured the fire and got revived; some of them were cut, their barks injured, some people pick up their leaves to make medicines for their sicknesses, birds used their leaves to make their nests, etc. Upon all these, the tree is still tree!

| *Israelmore Ayivor*

• *Forest of Mount Kinabalu, Borneo, Malaysia*

Chimpanzees, gorillas, orangutans
have been living for hundreds of
thousands of years in their forest, living
fantastic lives, never overpopulating,
never destroying the forest. I would
say that they have been in a way more
successful than us as far as being in
harmony with the environment.

| *Jane Goodall*

One thing leads to the other.
Deforestation leads to climate change,
which leads to ecosystem losses, which
negatively impacts our livelihoods—it's
a vicious cycle.

| *Gisele Bündchen*

If you can't excite people about wildlife, how can you convince them to love, cherish, and protect our wildlife and the environment they live in?

| *Steve Irwin*

232-233 • *Makahiku Falls, Maui, Hawaii (USA)* 233 • *Rainbow eucalyptus, Kauai, Hawaii (USA)*

Creating mechanisms for ending
deforestation and promoting
regeneration of the environment
is one of the most effective ways
of achieving net-zero emissions.

| *Guilherme Leal*

Cultivating and caring for creation is God's indication given to each one of us not only at the beginning of history; it is part of His project; it means nurturing the world with responsibility and transforming it into a garden, a habitable place for everyone.

| *Pope Francis*

• *Mont Tremblant National Park, Quebec, Canada*

Erosion of fertile topsoil, deforestation of our great forests, toxic air pollution, loss of insects and wildlife, the acidification of our oceans—these are all disastrous trends being accelerated by a way of life that we, here in our financially-fortunate part of the world, see as our right to simply carry on.

| *Greta Thunberg*

• *Giant sequoias, Redwood National and State Parks, California (USA)*

Swamp cypresses, Caddo Lake, Texas (USA)

240-241 • Monteverde Cloud Forest, Costa Rica 241 • Amazon tree boa, Monteverde Cloud Forest, Costa Rica

If all mankind were to disappear, the world would regenerate back to the rich state of equilibrium that existed ten thousand years ago. If insects were to vanish, the environment would collapse into chaos.

| *Edward Osborne Wilson*

We must protect the forests for our
children, grandchildren and children
yet to be born. We must protect the
forests for those who can't speak
for themselves such as the birds,
animals, fish and trees.

| *Qwatsinas*

242 left • Velvet-purple coronet, Ecuador 242 right • Plate-billed mountain toucan, Ecuador
243 • Mindo Cloud Forest, Ecuador

If we're destroying our trees and destroying our environment and hurting animals and hurting one another, there's got to be a very powerful energy to fight that. I think we need more love in the world. We need more kindness, more compassion, more joy, more laughter. I definitely want to contribute to that.

| *Ellen DeGeneres*

• *Amazon rainforest, Brazil*

At first I thought I was fighting to save
rubber trees, then I thought I was
fighting to save the Amazon rain forest.
Now I realize I am fighting for humanity.

| *Chico Mendes*

• *Amazon rainforest, Brazil*

When we can transcend our fear of the creatures of the forest, then we become one with all that is; we enter a unity of existence with our relatives—the animals, the plants and the land that sustains us.

| *Sylvia Dolson*

248 • Bald uakari, Brazil 248-249 • Blue-and-yellow macaw and scarlet macaw, Brazil

Glaciers

Disasters around the world are twice as big as they ever were, and ice is melting where it's not supposed to melt, and everything's changing— the world is changing—and it's all because of global warming.

| *Jerry Weintraub*

Expanses of white for as far as the eye can see and the mysterious lights of the Aurora Borealis, frozen seas where enormous towers of ice float slowly and relentlessly, skies where the sun never rises (or never sets), all surrounded by nothing but silence for thousands of miles. The Earth's largest deserts are not located in some sunny African or South American region. Actually, they are in the most diverse environment imaginable, beyond our planet's polar circles, where the ice is everlasting and the scarcity of precipitation impedes the growth of trees, and where the atmosphere is surreal and landscapes are both wondrous and unsettling.

The Arctic and Antarctic territories, situated at the north and south extremities of the Earth's axis, respectively, are incredibly harsh environments that have been explored on a

large scale only recently. The Arctic's relatively mild climate (temperatures range from -40°F [-40°C] in winter to 50°F [10°C] during the brief summer as opposed to temperatures lower than -112°F [-80°C] reported in Antarctica) has made it possible for nomadic populations such as the Inuit, Sami, and Yakut to establish themselves there. The first contact with Western man, which may have occurred during the (unconfirmed) voyage of the Greek explorer Pytheas in 325 BCE and subsequently during Viking expeditions in the 10th century, led to enduring ancient legends such as that of the Ultima Thule. Antarctica has also been an important presence in ancient history (Aristotle theorized the existence of a *Terra Australis* that would balance out the volume of the land in the Northern Hemisphere), but humans did not actually set foot there until 1821, and even now, the continent's population is limited to the guests of the few scientific bases located there. In both cases, exploring these frozen deserts took a high toll of human lives. The Scott expedition to the South Pole ended in tragedy in 1912, and the ships of Admiral Franklin that embarked on a mission to find the Northwest Passage disappeared into thin air, but other than the daring ventures associated with exploring the two continents, the Arctic and Antarctic are really two very different environments. The primary difference is geological: the Arctic is an ice pack surrounded by land (Alaska, Siberia, Canada, Greenland, Norway, and Iceland), while the Antarctic is a continent in and of itself, almost 25 times bigger than France. It is covered by a thick mantle of ice that makes it the continent with the most elevation, the average of which is 7,540 feet (2,300 m). Most of the fresh water reserves on the planet are located there.

These are not the only differences. The Arctic is home to large mammals like polar bears, reindeer, and caribou, while the Antarctic is the undisputed realm of marine fauna such as fish, cetaceans, and pinnipeds, and its only terrestrial fauna is limited to the birds that come there in summer to breed. The two continents are different from an administrative point of view as well. According to an international treaty adopted in 1959, the Antarctic does not belong to any country and it can be used exclusively for scientific research. Nonetheless, many international powers keep a close eye on the continent's mineral and oil deposits. The Arctic, on the other hand, has no ad hoc governing body. The geographic North Pole and the Arctic Ocean belong to international waters. Contiguous countries exercise their sovereignty over some areas claimed and are permitted to use their rich natural resources, especially oil and natural gas.

However, direct human exploitation is not the only threat to these extreme, precious ecosystems. In fact, global warming is eroding the ice caps at an unsustainable rate. The Arctic Ice Pack, which is thinner, more recent, and more easily melted, is taking the hardest blow. It is shrinking by an average of 20,810 square miles (53,900 square kilometers) a year and risks becoming an arctic sea with no ice in a few decades.

The situation is better in Antarctica. The currents here keep the warm waters of other oceans from reaching the continent and the rise in temperatures has provoked an increase in humidity and consequently, in snowfall, which has counterbalanced, at least in part, the loss of glacial mass. The continent is less threatened by the melting of its surface than it is by the constant detachment of increasingly large icebergs. According to research published in *Nature*, approximately 60% of the Antarctic's ice shelves are at risk of fracture. These changes are momentous and may become irreversible. If we want the poles as we know them to continue to exist, we have to act now.

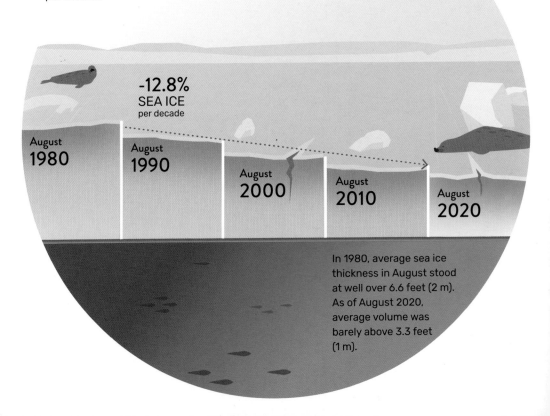

GLACIERS

Since 1980, the decline in the summer extent of Arctic sea ice has been **12.8%** per decade.

-12.8%
SEA ICE
per decade

August
1980

August
1990

August
2000

August
2010

August
2020

In 1980, average sea ice thickness in August stood at well over 6.6 feet (2 m). As of August 2020, average volume was barely above 3.3 feet (1 m).

Since 1979, the Arctic has lost, on average per year:

in Winter ·····>

13,000 mi²
(33,000 km²)
(Moldova's area)

in Summer ·····>

30,500 mi²
(79,000 km²)
(Scotland's area)

2000

Currently, the **Greenland Ice Sheet is losing ice mass** at an average rate that is almost four times higher than reported just 20 years ago.

2020

At the current rate of ice melt, Greenland is the largest contributor to global **sea level rise, increasing sea level .03 inch (.7 mm) per year.**

+.03 inch
(+.7 mm)

sea level rise per year

Temperature at the **top of the permafrost layer has increased by up to 5.4°F (3°C) since the 1980s** in the Arctic.

+5.4°F (+3°C)

top permafrost layer since the 1980s.

Sources:
Intergovernmental Panel on Climate Change (IPCC), NOAA's Arctic Program, National Snow & Ice Data Center, European Environment Agency

For humans, the Arctic is a harshly inhospitable place, but the conditions there are precisely what polar bears require to survive—and thrive. "Harsh" to us is "home" for them. Take away the ice and snow, increase the temperature by even a little, and the realm that makes their lives possible literally melts away.

| *Sylvia Earle*

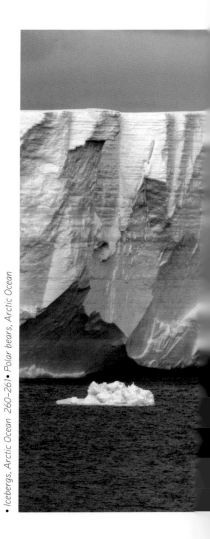

• Icebergs, Arctic Ocean 260–261• Polar bears, Arctic Ocean

In the Andes and the Alps, I have seen melting glaciers. At both of the Earth's Poles, I have seen open sea where ice once dominated the horizon.

| *Ban Ki-moon*

The entire North Polar ice cap is disappearing before our very eyes. It's been the size of the continental United States for the last 3 million years and now 40% is gone and the rest of it is going.

| *Al Gore*

• *Smeerenburg Glacier, Svalbard Islands, Norway*

Our own greed and stupidity are taking away the beautiful world of Arctic Ocean sea ice, which once protected us from the impacts of climatic extremes. Now urgent action is needed if we are to save ourselves from the consequences.

| *Peter Wadhams*

Global warming is one of those things, not like an earthquake where there's a big bang and you say, "Oh, my God, this is really, has hit us." It creeps up on you. Half a degree temperature difference from one year to the next, a little bit of rise of the ocean, a little bit of melting of the glaciers, and then all of a sudden it is too late to do something about it.

| *Arnold Schwarzenegger*

• *Norway*

Where the glacier meets the sky, the land ceases to be earthly, and the Earth becomes one with the heavens; no sorrows live there anymore, and therefore joy is not necessary; beauty alone reigns there, beyond all demands.

| *Halldór Laxness*

• *Baltic Sea*

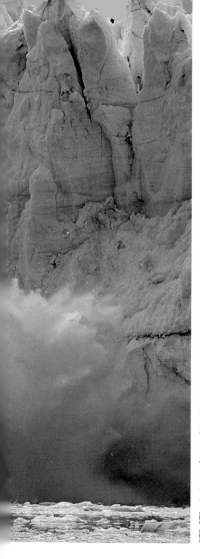

Future generations are not going to ask us what political party were you in. They are going to ask what did you do about it, when you knew the glaciers were melting.

| *Martin Sheen*

Our globe is under new dramatic
environmental pressure: our globe
is warming, our ice caps melting, our
glaciers receding, our coral is dying,
our soils are eroding, our water tables
falling, our fisheries are being depleted,
our remaining rainforests shrinking.
Something is very, very wrong with
our ecosystem.

| *Richard Lamm*

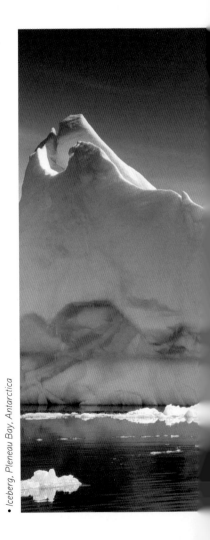

• *Iceberg, Pleneau Bay, Antarctica*

Antarctica Peninsula

We now know that we cannot continue to put ever-increasing amounts of carbon dioxide into the atmosphere. Actions have consequences. In fact, the consequences of past actions are already in the pipeline. Global temperatures are rising. Glaciers are melting. Sea levels are rising. Extreme weather events are multiplying.

| *Cary Fowler*

• *Iceberg, Antarctica*

• *Seal on an iceberg, Antarctica*

The last few years were the hottest on record. The loss of ice in Greenland and Antarctica is accelerating, meaning that sea levels will rise a full meter (over 3 feet) by 2100 if nothing is done to avoid it.

| *António Guterres*

• *Emperor penguins, Antarctica*

Savannas & Prairies

Today, more than ever before, life
must be characterized by a sense
of universal responsibility, not
only nation to nation and human
to human, but also human to other
forms of life.

| *Dalai Lama*

When you turn your television to any documentary channel, the scene you are most likely to find will be set in an African savanna, with lionesses hunting herds of gnus, majestic elephants spraying water from their trunks, and the typical silhouette of a giraffe against a red sunset on the horizon.

These are images we remember from our earliest childhood, and even though we have never set foot in these vast sunny grasslands, their landscape looks as familiar to us as the one surrounding our house.

These expanses of grasslands cover about one-fourth of the Earth's land surface. Their names vary according to the continent and the climate zone where they are located. In North

America they are the Great Plains, in northern Asia they are the steppes, in Africa they are savannas or "veldt," and in South America they are called "pampas" or "cerrados."

Grasslands occur in a specific climate that is too dry for trees to develop but humid enough that the territory does not become desertified. In tropical savannas, there may be abundant rain but it is concentrated in a single season so the plants and animals that live there must be specialized in order to survive the long periods of drought that follow the rainy season.

The level of plant biodiversity in these ecosystems is much higher than what it might seem at first glance. The grasslands in Patagonia, for example, are characterized by a great variety of plants, and in North America, in an area of just over 2.5 acres (1 ha) of grasslands, you can find up to 300 plant species that may host as many as 3 million individual insects in less than 1.2 acres (0.5 ha). There is also a very high degree of animal biodiversity, including numerous species of reptiles and invertebrates and, above all, mammals of all sizes. The readily available herbaceous plants in the savanna make it the perfect home for these great herbivores. This kind of vegetation regenerates season after season while the animals migrate to ungrazed areas, leaving time for the grasses to grow again. The great herds of buffalo and wild horses that galloped in Europe and North America are now only a distant memory, but in the African savannas, there is still a high density of grazing animals such as gnus, zebras, and antelopes, as well as the "giants" such as elephants and rhinoceroses, which, however, are on the brink of extinction. Wherever there are large concentrations of herbivores, there will also be their predators, such as lions, leopards, cheetahs, and hyenas.

But the one primary predator in this kind of ecosystem is always the same—man. With large scale colonization in North America, the prairies of the "Wild West" became fields and pastures that almost completely swept away much of the fauna typical to the area, such as the bison. The same thing is happening in some of the densely populated areas of Africa, particularly in Sudan and the Sahel. Here, the communities of herders used to move with their herds from season to season, but an explosive increase in population combined with measures taken by the government to limit nomadism have led to the excessive exploitation of some areas, and the creation of new wells has led to an uncontrolled increase in the number of animals being raised. The savanna in Sudan and the Sahel has been dramatically changed by human activity. The reduction of vegetation cover in these regions has resulted in the serious impoverishment of the soil, which in turn leads to famine, particularly when the seasonal rainfall is scarce. Hunting has also taken a heavy toll on the environmental equilibrium of the savanna, in some cases causing the complete disappearance of animals such as elephants and rhinoceroses that are killed for their tusks and horns. The network of national parks in Africa guarantees some protection, but unfortunately, poaching is still practiced widely, sometimes inside the parks themselves.

The Brazilian Cerrado is the most biodiverse savanna in the world and is home to 5% of the species on Earth. Nonetheless, it is also receiving lethal blows from intensive farming. Approximately half of its original surface area has already been transformed into plantations of soy, mostly destined for the European market, and just between January and April of 2021, another 14.5 square miles (3,774 ha) were destroyed, almost twice the surface area of London.

The situation is quite serious. We may hear about it and fear it less than deforestation, but the loss of grasslands would be just as disastrous for the planet. It would accelerate desertification, which would lead to the extinction of innumerable species. Once again, we have to realize that the time has come to do everything we can to reverse the situation, before it is too late.

SAVANNAS & PRAIRIES

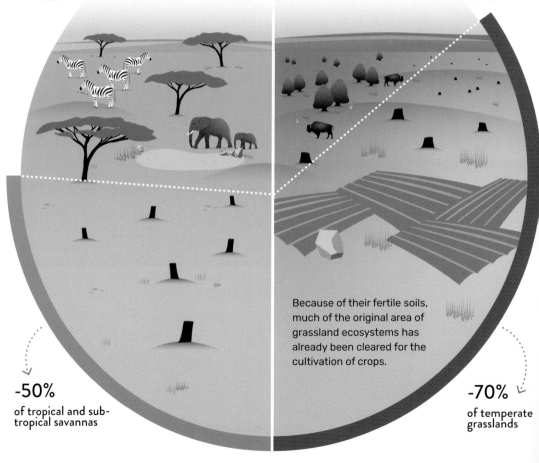

Because of their fertile soils, much of the original area of grassland ecosystems has already been cleared for the cultivation of crops.

-50%
of tropical and sub-tropical savannas

-70%
of temperate grasslands

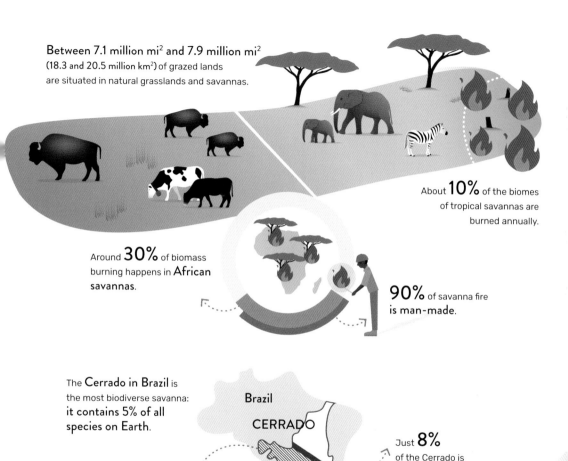

Between 7.1 million mi^2 and 7.9 million mi^2 (18.3 and 20.5 million km^2) of grazed lands are situated in natural grasslands and savannas.

About **10%** of the biomes of tropical savannas are burned annually.

Around **30%** of biomass burning happens in **African savannas**.

90% of savanna fire is man-made.

The **Cerrado in Brazil** is the most biodiverse savanna: **it contains 5% of all species on Earth**.

Brazil

CERRADO

Just **8%** of the Cerrado is legally protected.

50% of the Cerrado has already been cleared for agriculture expansion.

Sources: WWF, Convention on Biological Diversity, IPCC Special Report on Climate Change and Land, Encyclopedia of Environmental Health

Nothing is more important than saving . . . the lions, tigers, giraffes, elephants, froggies, turtles, apes, raccoons, beetles, ants, sharks, bears, and, of course, the squirrels. The humans? The planet does not need humans.

| *James Lee*

• Wildebeests, Masai Mara National Park, Kenya
294–295 • African elephants, Tanzania

We admire elephants in part because they demonstrate what we consider the finest human traits: empathy, self-awareness, and social intelligence. But the way we treat them puts on display the very worst of human behavior.

| *Graydon Carter*

• Kola Peninsula, Russia

• Tundra, Russia

We are in danger of destroying ourselves by our greed and stupidity. We cannot remain looking inwards at ourselves on a small and increasingly polluted and overcrowded planet.

| *Stephen Hawking*

Something will have gone out of us
as a people if we permit the last virgin
forests to be turned into comic books
and plastic cigarette cases; if we drive
the few remaining members of the wild
species into zoos or to extinction; if we
pollute the last clear air and dirty the
last clean streams and push our paved
roads through the last of the silence.

| *Wallace Stegner*

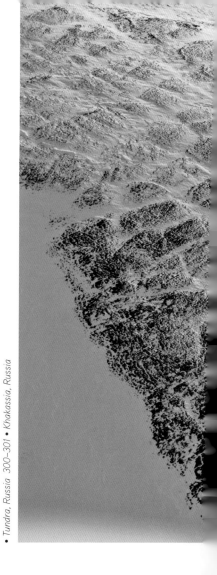

• Tundra, Russia 300–301 • Khakassia, Russia

Wildlife is something which man cannot construct. Once it is gone, it is gone forever. Man can rebuild a pyramid, but he can't rebuild ecology, or a giraffe.

| *Joy Adamson*

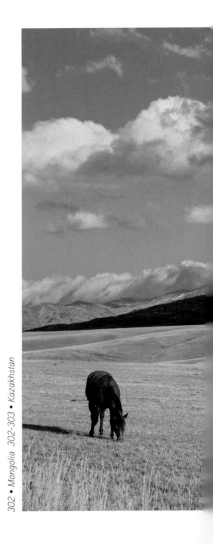

Economic desperation often drives wildlife destruction like poaching or illegal logging. But trade can help create powerful financial incentives for communities to preserve the biodiversity around them.

| *Arancha González*

• *Outback, Australia*

Alive, the grizzly is a symbol of freedom and understanding—a sign that man can learn to conserve what is left of the Earth. Extinct, it will be another fading testimony to things man should have learned more about but was too preoccupied with himself to notice. A symbol of what man is doing to the entire planet.

| *Frank Craighead*

306-307 • *Denali National Park, Alaska (USA)* 307 • *Grizzly bear, Denali National Park, Alaska (USA)*

• *American bison, South Dakota (USA)*

The single biggest threat to our planet is the destruction of habitat and along the way loss of precious wildlife. We need to reach a balance where people, habitat, and wildlife can co-exist—if we don't everyone loses . . . one day.

| *Steve Irwin*

Being a vegetarian allows you to live better and avoid animal suffering. Intensive farming is now the main source of pollution. Limit the consumption of animal products would do right both to environment and to animals, many of which are by now reduced to meat producing machines.

| *Margherita Hack*

• *Gran Sabana, Venezuela*

312-313 • *Altiplano, Bolivia* 313 • *Vicunas, Altiplano, Bolivia* 314-315 • *Patagonia, Argentina*

All over the world the wildlife that
I write about is in grave danger.
It is being exterminated by what we
call the progress of civilization.

| *Gerald Durrell*

Fresh Water

Only when the last tree has died

and the last river has been poisoned

and the last fish been caught will

we realize we cannot eat money.

| *Cree Indian Prophecy*

Regardless of eras, climates, latitudes, and longitudes, there has been one single common denominator in determining the birth of human settlements in the various parts of the world—the presence of a large river: the Nile River in Egypt, the Euphrates River in Mesopotamia, the Indus and Ganges Rivers in India, and the Yellow and Yangtze Rivers in China. For thousands of years, these important waterways witnessed the growth and prosperity of human settlements that developed into powerful cities and empires over time.

The reason is very simple: fresh water is without a doubt the most important resource for guaranteeing the existence of life on Earth. It was from the primordial soup that the first single cell beings were born, and even millions of years later, all existing life forms, from the

sequoia to the ant, need water to "function." Even the specialized organisms that live in the desert have to know how to find and use the little humidity that is available in order to survive.

Obviously, humans are no exception. Most of us have heard it said that a healthy person can survive for weeks without eating but only for three days without drinking. It is no surprise that in prehistoric times, with the end of nomadism and the advent of agriculture, the availability of fresh water was the primary prerequisite for settling in one area rather than in another. The water from a river or lake was essential, not only for drinking but also for washing, cooking, irrigating, and watering the animals, and since there were no roads, waterways were the only means of transportation and contact with other populations.

Fresh water is extremely precious, not only for its fundamental usefulness but also because it is much scarcer than it seems. Our planet is literally covered with water (approximately 71% of its surface), but over 97% of that water is salt water and therefore unusable. Of the small amount remaining, 70% is blocked in glaciers and polar caps. Only a minimal percentage circulates freely in the so-called "wet regions." Despite their limited size, rivers, lakes, and swamps are among the most biodiverse environments with over 40% of the world's species of fish. They provide a number of ecosystem services, such as the regulation of hydrogeological cycles and carbon fixation in the biosphere.

Looking at the global picture, our fresh water, a scarce, vital resource, seems to be barely enough to meet the needs of life on the planet and of humans in particular. Unfortunately, this impression is not far from being accurate. In fact, at least 70% of available fresh water is currently being used for intensive agriculture and animal farming. It is estimated that 340 gallons (1,300 L) of water are needed to produce 2.2 pounds (1 kg) of wheat, 900 gallons (3,400 L) for 2.2 pounds (1 kg) of rice, and no less than 4,200 gallons (16,000 L) for 2.2 pounds (1 kg) of beef. In addition to large-scale consumption, the unjustifiable waste on the part of individuals has a much more serious effect than you might think. For example, if you leave the water running while you brush your teeth, you can waste as much as 1.8 gallons (7 L) of drinking water a day. According to a study published by NASA, between 2003 and 2013, a third of all of the Earth's aquifers showed signs of depletion. Where water is still available, pollution often intervenes and compromises its quality; in Europe alone, as much as 60% of the wet regions fail to meet "good status" standards, and the situation in the rest of the world is even worse. Large lakes like Lake Baikal in Russia (the deepest on the planet) are polluted with wastewater that kills fish and favors the proliferation of algae, while others, such as Lake Chad in Africa, are drying up because of excessive extraction and careless government management. According to National Geographic, approximately 20% of species of freshwater fish are at risk or have already become extinct, and a WWF study confirms that ten of the Earth's largest rivers are in grave danger caused by pollution and climate change as well as by the construction of dykes, navigation, irresponsible fishing, and the spread of invasive species.

In addition, global warming is modifying hydrogeological cycles and making arid regions more arid and wet regions wetter. In some areas of the world, hurricanes and other weather events are becoming increasingly more frequent and destructive, and in others, in a not too distant future, desertification could lead to veritable thirst wars.

So now, more than ever, fresh water is a resource that must be protected because tomorrow, we may no longer be able to take that cool stream of water that flows from our faucets for granted.

FRESH WATER

Tropical cyclone intensities globally are projected to increase on average by 1 to 10% according to model projections for a 3.6°F (2°C) global warming.

Increase for rainfall rates
10–15%*

*within about **62 miles** (100 km) of the storm

For a global warming scenario of **+3.6°F** (**+2°C**)

1–10%
Tropical cyclone intensity increase

Once one of Africa's largest lakes, **Lake Chad has shrunk by around 90%** since the 1960s.

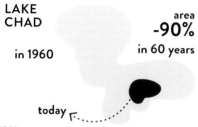

LAKE CHAD
in 1960

area -90%
in 60 years

today

CAUSES:
- reduction of precipitation
- development of modern irrigation systems for agriculture
- increasing human demand for fresh water

Lake Poopó, Bolivia's second-largest lake just a few decades ago, in its wet season peak stretched almost 43 miles (70 km) in length and covered an area of 1,160 mi² (3,000 km²).
The lake dried out entirely at the end of 2015. Many of the lake's **200 animal species** disappeared.

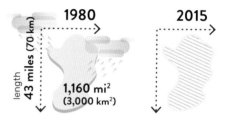

1980

2015

length 43 miles (70 km)

1,160 mi² (3,000 km²)

temperature
+2.2°F (+1.2°C)

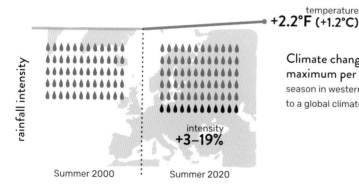

rainfall intensity

intensity
+3–19%

Summer 2000

Summer 2020

Climate change increased the intensity of the maximum per day rainfall event in the summer season in western Europe by **about 3–19%** compared to a global climate 2.2°F (1.2°C) cooler than today.

In Europe, 60% of rivers, lakes, and wetlands currently fail to meet the "good status" requirement of the EU's water legislation.

bad status
60%

good status
40%

Sources: European Space Agency, European Environment Agency, EU Water Framework Directive (WFD), Geophysical Fluid Dynamics Laboratory, Intergovernmental Panel on Climate Change (IPCC)

Anything else you're interested in is not going to happen if you can't breathe the air and drink the water. Don't sit this one out. Do something. You are by accident of fate alive at an absolutely critical moment in the history of our planet.

| *Carl Sagan*

• Godafoss, Iceland

The truth is: the natural world is changing. And we are totally dependent on that world. It provides our food, water and air. It is the most precious thing we have and we need to defend it.

| *Sir David Attenborough*

• Plitvice Lakes, Croatia

The difference between animals
and humans is that animals change
themselves for the environment,
but humans change the environment
for themselves.

| *Ayn Rand*

• *Danube River, Romania*

Sustainability is not just about adopting the latest energy-efficient technologies or turning to renewable sources of power. Sustainability is the responsibility of every individual every day. It is about changing our behavior and mindset to reduce power and water consumption, thereby helping to control emissions and pollution levels.

| *Joe Kaeser*

No matter who we are or where
we come from, we're all entitled to
the basic human rights of clean air
to breathe, clean water to drink,
and healthy land to call home.

| *Martin Luther King III*

• Victoria Falls, Zambia/Zimbabwe/South Africa

335

Our rivers are polluted by an incredible
variety of waste, domestic, chemical,
radioactive, so that our planet, although
dominated by the seas that cover three
quarters of its surface, it is becoming
a thirsty world.

| *Rachel Carson*

• *Okavango Delta, Botswana*

I understood when I was just a child
that without water, everything dies.
I didn't understand until much later that
no one "owns" water. It might rise on
your property, but it just passes through.
You can use it, and abuse it, but it is
not yours to own. It is part of the global
commons, not "property" but part
of our life support system.

| *Marq de Villiers*

• *Ganges River, Uttarakhand, India*

For many of us, water simply flows from a faucet, and we think little about it beyond this point of contact. We have lost a sense of respect for the wild river, for the complex workings of a wetland, for the intricate web of life that water supports.

| *Sandra Postel*

Yangtze River, China

Mekong River, Thailand

Man is endowed with reason and
the power to create, so that he may
increase that which has been given
him, but until now he has not created,
but demolished. The forests are
disappearing, the rivers are running
dry, the wild life is exterminated,
the climate is spoiled, and the Earth
becomes poorer and uglier every day.

| *Anton Chekhov*

For many of us, clean water is so plentiful and readily available that we rarely, if ever, pause to consider what life would be like without it.

| *Marcus Samuelsson*

344 • Barron Falls, Queensland, Australia 344-345 • Bloomfield River, Queensland, Australia

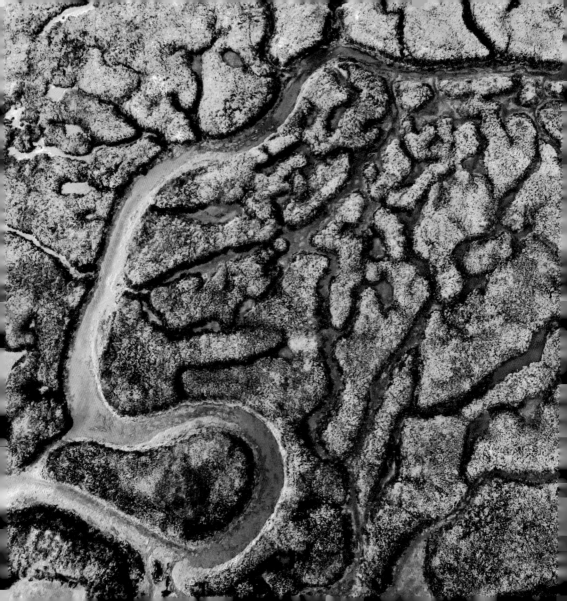

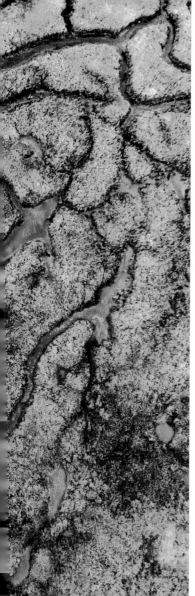

All living beings, things that move,
are equally important, whether they are
human beings, dogs, birds, fish, trees,
ants, weeds, rivers, wind or rain.
To stay healthy and strong, life must
have clean air, clear water and pure
food. If deprived of these things,
life will cycle to the next level, or as
the system says, "die."

| *John Africa*

Water is one of the most basic of all
needs—we cannot live for more than
a few days without it. And yet, most
people take water for granted. We waste
water needlessly and don't realize that
clean water is a very limited resource.

| *Robert Alan Aurthur*

No water, no life. No blue, no green. It is the worst of times but it is the best of times because we still have a chance. Many of us ask what can I, as one person, do, but history shows us that everything good and bad starts because somebody does something or does not do something.

| *Sylvia Earle*

• *Niagara Falls, USA/Canada*

• Bayou, Mississippi River, Louisiana (USA)

We have the ability to provide clean
water for every man, woman and child
on the Earth. What has been lacking
is the collective will to accomplish this.
What are we waiting for? This is the
commitment we need to make
to the world, now.

| *Jean-Michel Cousteau*

356 • American alligator, Everglades National Park, Florida (USA) 356-357 • Everglades National Park, Florida (USA)

We still think of air as free. But clean
air is not free, and neither is clean
water. The price tag on pollution control
is high. Through our years of past
carelessness we incurred a debt to
nature, and now that debt is being called.

| *Richard Nixon*

Angel Falls, Venezuela

It's amazing how people can get so
excited about a rocket to the moon and
not give a damn about smog, oil leaks,
the devastation of the environment
with pesticides, hunger, disease. When
the poor share some of the power that
the affluent now monopolize, we will
give a damn.

| *César Chávez*

• *Amazon River, Brazil*

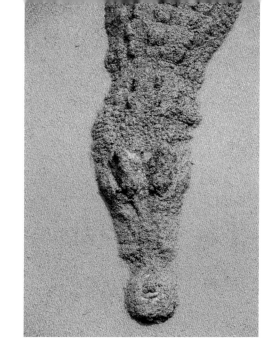

362-363 • Water lilies (Victoria amazonica), Amazon River, Peru 363 • Black caiman, Amazon River, Peru

The need for clean water knows
no borders, and proper management
and intervention can be a currency for
peace and international cooperation.

| *Bill Frist*

364-365 • Water hyacinth, Pantanal, Brazil 365 top • Jabiru stork, Pantanal, Brazil 365 bottom • Capybara, Pantanal, Brazil

Wildlife of the world is disappearing,
not because of a malicious and
deliberate policy of slaughter and
extermination, but simply because
of a general and widespread ignorance
and neglect.

| *Prince Philip, Duke of Edinburgh*

Poverty feeds into the clean-water crisis, which contributes to hunger, and so on. There's undeniable interconnectivity among these issues. Just one of these problems can be deadly on its own, but in the most disadvantaged areas there is a perfect storm of problems. And it takes its greatest toll on children.

| *Matt Damon*

Must we always teach our children with books? Let them look at the stars and the mountains above. Let them look at the waters and the trees and flowers on Earth. Then they will begin to think, and to think is the beginning of a real education.

| *David Polis*

• *Iguazu Falls, Argentina/Brazil*

Volcanoes

The question is not "can you make a difference?" You already do make a difference. It's just a matter of what kind of difference you want to make during your life on this planet.

| *Julia Hill*

Between 1816 and 1818, the world was struck by a series of disastrous events that shaped the course of history. Summers became cold and precipitation was abnormal. Red snow fell in Italy. In Germany, floods killed herds of livestock, and in Ireland, potatoes rotted in the soil, as did the rice in the Yunnan valleys. The cooling of the waters in the Bay of Bengal, the habitat of the cholera bacteria, produced a more aggressive pathogenic strain that caused a pandemic like no other before it. The famine and disease that took a heavy toll on a Europe already suffering from years of Napoleonic wars provoked unrest and revolt. Thousands of people migrated to the United States, which turned out to be a bad idea since conditions were more or less the same. Crops had been destroyed and fodder was in short supply, so animal farmers were

  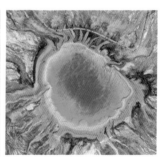

forced to embark on the great race toward the West, a mass exodus that caused the population in Ohio to double and that in Indiana to quadruple in just three years. Artists of the period, such as Friedrich and Turner, portrayed the disquieting, gloomy light and the heavy clouds that darkened the skies of Europe, creating the philosophical concept of the "sublime," the bewilderment that man experiences when faced with the power of nature. During long, bleak, rainy stays, authors such as John William Polidori and Mary Shelley conceived the stories of monsters and vampires that would become the foundation of Gothic literature, while in Italy, the young poet Leopardi wrote about the mockery of "stepmother nature."

The oddest thing is that the lives of all these people, from the poorest Chinese farmer to the romantic German painter, were affected by weather phenomena that originated from a single event that occurred thousands of miles away, an event that none of them could have ever imagined. It all began in April 1815. In the western world, very few people had heard of the volcano Mount Tambora in faraway Indonesia, but it was the eruption of that obscure volcano, the most powerful in 10,000 years, that devastated the planet. The volcano caused incalculable damages in the surrounding area: the destruction of three kingdoms, 100,000 victims, and a tsunami that traveled for more than 750 miles (1,200 km). Additionally, the clouds and debris it released into the atmosphere provoked what climatologists call a mini ice age—years with no summer.

Volcanoes are actually the most powerful and fearsome geological structures on the planet. They are fractures in the Earth's crust from which masses of molten rock, gases, and dust rise, sometimes gradually and sometimes explosively. They are capable of modifying climates and ecosystems, even those that are far away, in both negative and positive ways. Apart from the immediate catastrophes, eruptions also produce volcanic ash, which is a source of life, an extraordinary fertilizer that increases the quality and quantity of crops, even at a great distance from the volcano itself. For thousands of years, the richness of the soil that results has led people to live on the slopes of volcanoes despite the risk.

Very recent studies have also shown that volcanic activity makes a fundamental contribution to conserving the atmosphere. In the fractures between the tectonic plates, over 16,400 feet (5,000 m) below the surface, gigantic ecosystems of microbes thrive. They feed on the chemicals produced by subduction, capturing a large amount of carbon that would otherwise escape into the atmosphere. They act as a kind of "underground forest," which, instead of using sunlight for photosynthesis, uses chemicals of volcanic origin.

Volcanoes are important for the balance of the planet and they create spectacular landscapes, but above all, they make us shudder with fear. The energy they hide in their depths is a bomb waiting to go off, capable of causing damages that range from disrupting air traffic, as with the eruption of Eyjafjallajökull in Iceland in 2010, to disaster of biblical proportions that would occur if a supervolcano like the Yellowstone Caldera erupted.

Yet, this catastrophic power is put into perspective if we compare it to the damage that humans, on their own, are capable of causing the environment. The environmental impact of a volcano like Tambora, or more recently the Pinatubo in the Philippines, is lower than the gradual global warming caused by human activity. It is estimated that the level of carbon dioxide emissions caused by humans is more than 35 times that produced by all the active volcanoes on Earth. Think about that the next time news of an eruption, somewhere in the world, fills the front pages of our newspapers.

VOLCANOES

0.13–0.44 Gt
Volcanic activity

35 Gt
Human
activity

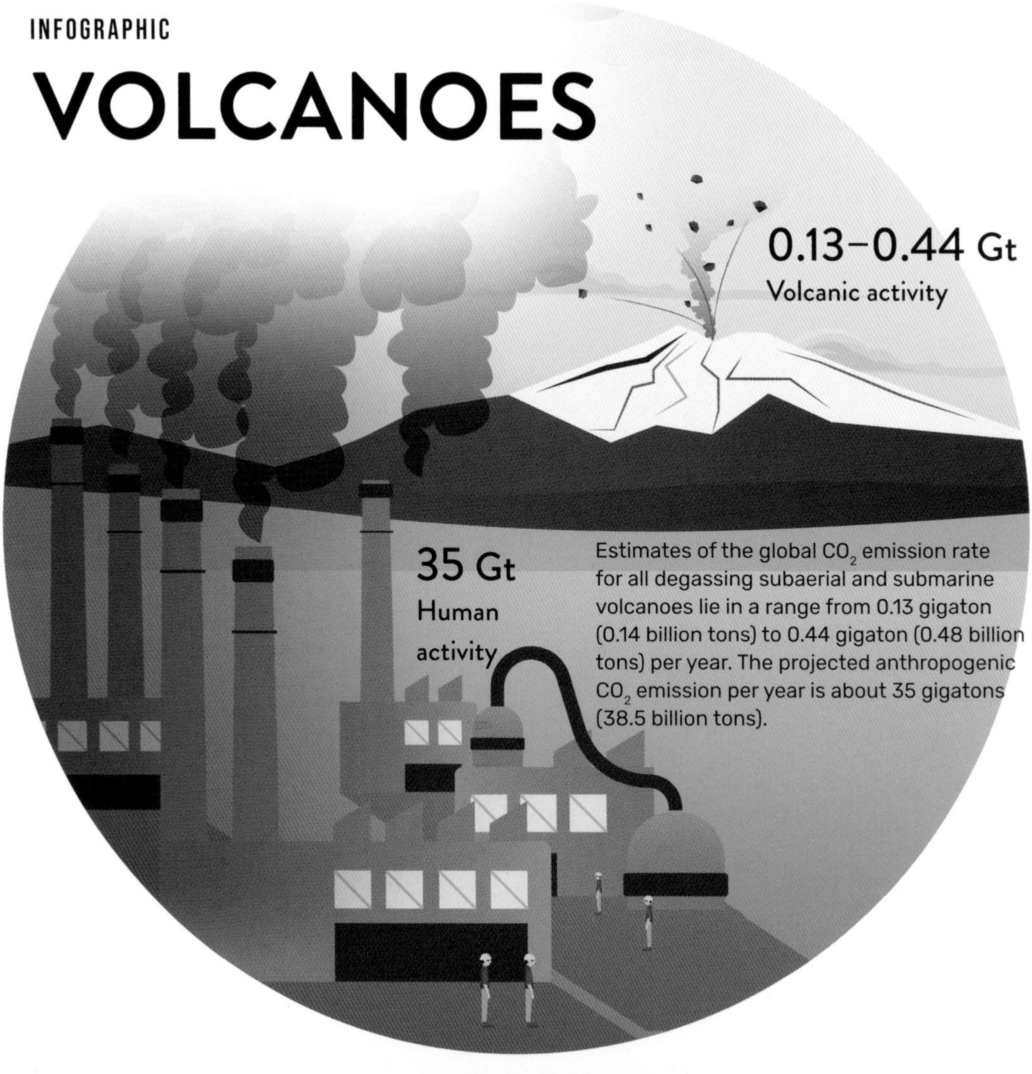

Estimates of the global CO_2 emission rate for all degassing subaerial and submarine volcanoes lie in a range from 0.13 gigaton (0.14 billion tons) to 0.44 gigaton (0.48 billion tons) per year. The projected anthropogenic CO_2 emission per year is about 35 gigatons (38.5 billion tons).

The climactic eruption of **Mount Pinatubo (Philippines)** on June 15, 1991, caused what is believed to be the largest aerosol disturbance of the stratosphere in the twentieth century. Consequently, it was a standout in its climate impact and cooled Earth's surface for three years following the eruption, by as much as .9°F (.5° C). **The average global temperature on Earth has increased by a little more than 1.8°F (1°C) since 1880, as a consequence of human activity.**

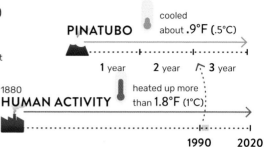

PINATUBO — cooled about .9°F (.5°C)

1 year   2 year   3 year

1880
HUMAN ACTIVITY — heated up more than 1.8°F (1°C)

1990   2020

1980
MOUNT ST. HELENS
11,000,000 t (10,000,000 metric t) CO_2
1 h   2 h   3 h   4 h   5 h   6 h   7 h   8 h   9 h

HUMAN ACTIVITY
11,000,000 t (10,000,000 metric t) CO_2
1 h   2 h   3 h   4 h   5 h   6 h   7 h   8 h   9 h

The 1980 **eruption of Mount St. Helens** (Washington, USA) vented approximately 11 millions tons (10 million metric tons) of CO_2 into the atmosphere in only 9 hours. However, it currently takes humanity only 2.5 hours to put out the same amount.

Global warming will also accelerate the transport of volcanic material to higher layers of the atmosphere.
For large eruptions, the combined effect of these phenomena will ultimately **amplify by 15% the temporary cooling caused by volcanic eruptions.** However, the cooling effects of small- and medium-sized eruptions could shrink by as much as 75%.

-75%
effects of temporary cooling for small- and medium-sized eruptions

+15%
effects of temporary cooling for large eruptions

TEMPORARY COOLING

Sources: U.S. Geological Survey, Nature Communications

Bardarbunga volcano, Iceland

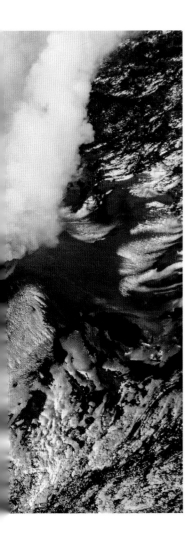

The fact that a cloud from a minor
volcanic eruption in Iceland—a small
disturbance in the complex mechanism
of life on the Earth—can bring
to a standstill the aerial traffic over
an entire continent is a reminder
of how, with all its power to transform
nature, humankind remains just
another species on the planet Earth.

| *Slavoj Žižek*

• *Etna volcano, Sicily, Italy*

For most of history, man has had to fight
nature to survive; in this century
he is beginning to realize that, in order
to survive, he must protect it.

| *Jacques-Yves Cousteau*

We abuse land because we regard
it as a commodity belonging to us.
When we see land as a community
to which we belong, we may begin
to use it with love and respect.

| *Aldo Leopold*

382 • Mount Kilimanjaro, Tanzania
383 • Mount Nyiragongo, Dem. Rep. of Congo

Pollution is nothing but the resources
we are not harvesting. We allow them
to disperse because we've been ignorant
of their value.

| *Richard Buckminster Fuller*

There is hardly a place on Earth where people do not log, pave, spray, drain, flood, graze, fish, plow, burn, drill, spill or dump. There is no life zone, with the possible exception of the deep ocean, that we are not degrading.

| *Donella Meadows*

• *Mount Fuji, Japan*

All Nature's wildness tells the same
story: the shocks and outbursts of
earthquakes, volcanoes, geysers,
roaring, thundering waves and floods,
the silent uprush of sap in plants,
storms of every sort, each and all,
are the orderly, beauty-making love-beats
of Nature's heart.

| *John Muir*

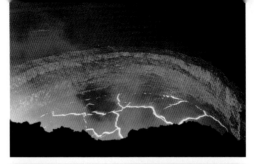

It is our collective and individual
responsibility to protect and nurture
the global family, to support its weaker
members and to preserve and tend
to the environment in which we all live.

| *Dalai Lama*

• Mount Saint Helens, Washington (USA)

The environment and the economy are
really both two sides of the same coin.
If we cannot sustain the environment,
we cannot sustain ourselves.

| *Wangari Maathai*

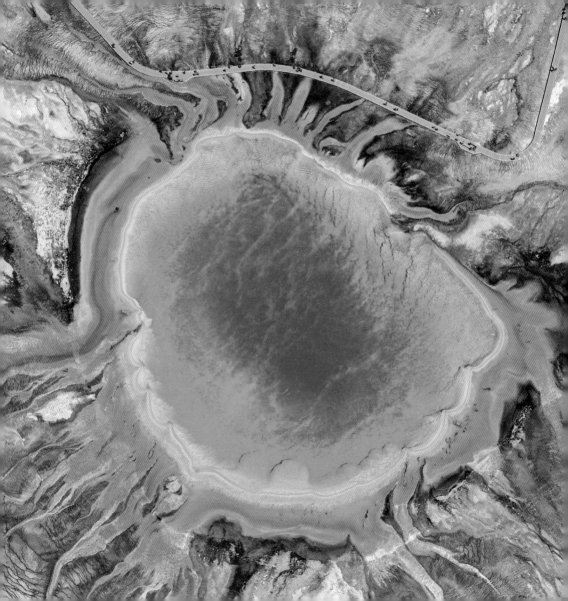

It suddenly struck me that that tiny pea, pretty and blue, was the Earth. I put up my thumb and shut one eye, and my thumb blotted out the planet Earth. I didn't feel like a giant. I felt very, very small.

| *Neil Armstrong*

Authors

ELENA ROSSI is a journalist and translator. She has collaborated with monthly and online publications on the subjects of history, art, and the environment. She has translated photography manuals for White Star Publishers and publications for National Geographic. She wrote the introduction to this book.

ILARIA GHISLETTI earned her degree in economics and management of cultural assets at Catholic University in Milan, with a thesis on geographic information systems applied to tourism. She has worked in publishing since 2013 as an editor and translator. She wrote the introductory texts of the chapters.

Photo Credits

COVER: Zhangye Danxia Landform Geopark, Gansu, China (Hiddenchina/Shutterstock)
BACK COVER: Mount Field National Park, Tasmania, Australia (MrForever/Shutterstock)

All images are from Shutterstock.com except: page 5, Bernardo Galmarini/Alamy Foto Stock; pages 70–71, Nicolas Daumas/EyeEm/Getty Images; pages 272–273, Paul Souders/Getty Images; pages 346–347, Artur Debat/Getty Images; page 382, Friedrich von Hörsten/Alamy Foto Stock; page 383, robertharding/Alamy Foto Stock; page 391, Jim Sugar/Getty Images

Infographics by Bianco Tangerine

Text
Elena Rossi
Ilaria Ghisletti

Project editor
Valeria Manferto De Fabianis

Editorial assistant
Giorgio Ferrero

Graphic design
Paola Piacco

WS White Star Publishers® is a registered trademark property of White Star s.r.l.

© 2022 White Star s.r.l.
Piazzale Luigi Cadorna, 6 - 20123 Milan, Italy
www.whitestar.it

Translation: Iceigeo, Milano (Cynthia Anne Koeppe)
Editing: Abby Young

ISBN 978-88-544-1872-1
1 2 3 4 5 6   26 25 24 23 22

Printed in China

MIX
Paper from
responsible sources
FSC® C019238